FOUNDATIONS OF MODERN POLITICAL SCIENCE SERIES

Robert A. Dahl, Editor

THE AGE OF IDEOLOGY—POLITICAL THOUGHT, 1750 TO THE PRESENT,
Second Edition
by Frederick M. Watkins

THE AMERICAN PARTY SYSTEM AND THE AMERICAN PEOPLE, Second Edition
by Fred I. Greenstein

THE ANALYSIS OF INTERNATIONAL RELATIONS
by Karl W. Deutsch

COMPARATIVE GOVERNMENT
by Dankwart A. Rustow

CONGRESS AND THE PRESIDENCY, Second Edition
by Nelson W. Polsby

DATA ANALYSIS IN POLITICAL SCIENCE
by Edward R. Tufte

INTEREST-GROUPS
by Graham Wootton

JUDICIAL BEHAVIOR
by David J. Danelski

MODERN POLITICAL ANALYSIS, Second Edition
by Robert A. Dahl

NORMATIVE POLITICAL THEORY
by Fred M. Frohock

PERSPECTIVES IN CONSTITUTIONAL LAW, with Revisions
by Charles L. Black, Jr.

THE POLICY-MAKING PROCESS
by Charles E. Lindblom

POLITICS AND POLICIES IN STATE AND LOCAL GOVERNMENTS
by Herbert Kaufman

PUBLIC ADMINISTRATION
by James W. Fesler

PUBLIC OPINION
by Robert E. Lane and David O. Sears

SYSTEMS OF POLITICAL SCIENCE
by Oran R. Young

READINGS IN AMERICAN POLITICAL BEHAVIOR, Second Edition
edited by Raymond E. Wolfinger

READINGS IN MODERN POLITICAL ANALYSIS, Second Edition
edited by Deane E. Neubauer

READINGS ON STATE AND LOCAL GOVERNMENT
edited by Irwin N. Gertzog

READINGS ON THE INTERNATIONAL POLITICAL SYSTEM
edited by Naomi Rosenbaum

FOUNDATIONS OF MODERN POLITICAL SCIENCE SERIES

PRENTICE-HALL, INC., Englewood Cliffs, New Jersey

NORMATIVE POLITICAL THEORY

FRED M. FROHOCK

Syracuse University

Library of Congress Cataloging in Publication Data

FROHOCK, FRED M
    Normative political theory. *see slip*

    (Foundations of modern political science series)
    Includes bibliographies.
    1. Political ethics. 2. Political science.
I. Title.
JA79.F73   320'.01   73–10027
ISBN 0–13-623710–X (pbk.)
ISBN 0–13-623728–2 (case)

FOUNDATIONS OF MODERN POLITICAL SCIENCE SERIES

Robert A. Dahl, Editor

NORMATIVE POLITICAL THEORY
by Fred M. Frohock

PRENTICE-HALL INTERNATIONAL, INC., London
PRENTICE-HALL OF AUSTRALIA, PTY. LTD., Sydney
PRENTICE-HALL OF CANADA, LTD., Toronto
PRENTICE-HALL OF INDIA PRIVATE LIMITED, New Delhi
PRENTICE-HALL OF JAPAN, INC., Tokyo

10 9 8 7 6 5 4 3 2 1

To Renée and Christina

CONTENTS

CHAPTER FIVE

MORALITY AND SOCIETY

INDEX

PREFACE

No one who has been connected with education the last several years can have failed to discuss "values" in one way or another. The issues of academic freedom, research objectivity, student and scholar participation in politics, that abused term "relevance"—all these and many more have recently become fashionable concerns for students and teachers alike. What is not often grasped is that these issues have philosophical roots which must be unearthed if the issues are to be discussed sensibly. It is a melancholy fact of language that even so urgent a word as "relevance" reverts quickly back to the reflective question "What *is* relevance?"—a philosophical inquiry.

It would be a mistake to think that all disagreements on "social" issues would disappear if we could get our philosophies in order (assuming that we could even do that). There is no hard and straight line connecting philosophical ideas to social concerns such that a stand on something like "relevance" can be deduced from a philosophical thesis. Anyone who has read or argued philosophy, no matter the level, has discovered that truth. But it is also clear that the more urgent issues of the day cannot escape their philosophical underpinnings. Discussing them in depth is like embarking on a journey—try it and see—in which the terrain gradually, and sometimes quickly, changes beyond recognition. From topics like academic freedom, research objectivity, we find ourselves in an area of truth claims, rules of inference, definitional criteria.

"Why is this so?" is a question often impatiently asked. If asked by someone more responsible for action than reflection, the question is eminently reasonable, especially in the face of the concession that philosophical discussions will not necessarily lead to any conclusions, may in fact introduce their own problems. The answer, in part, is a statement on what is required in any inquiry. To make a claim, as opposed to screaming, grunting, fighting, is to assert something which is bound by the rules of discourse. These rules stand, like a shadow on a bright day, directly connected to the claim. When the claim is a matter of dispute, when it is an issue, then the question of its truth or validity is at stake. *This* question then automatically invokes the rules, makes the shadow the subject; for it is impossible to say how one's claim is true, or justifiable, without entering a discussion of what truth or justification are.

It follows that philosophy, while not guaranteed to settle anything, will at least clarify the criteria by which claims can be settled. Without such reflection, what might be called a look at second-order ideas like inference and evidence, one cannot be clear just what is at stake in a discussion. Worst of all to the activist, time may be wasted over unimportant or confused items. There is no point trying to defend philosophy, or any reflective activity, as a foolproof way to save time. But it is helpful to locate accurately what may really be at stake below the surface of an argument, and what it will take to reach an agreement if one is possible. And at least time isn't wasted, if it isn't actually saved.

The reader will look in vain for an explicit treatment of current issues in the pages which follow. But the pages are filled with the philosophical foundation on which these issues are founded. Chapter One is a discussion of neutrality in social inquiry through an examination of the Weber-Strauss differences. Chapter Two explores some recent attempts to identify a necessary connection between evaluative and descriptive statements. Chapter Three examines the possibility that law may furnish grounds for deriving *ought* from *is,* and discusses the possibility that law is by definition fused with morality. Chapter Four develops a definition of morality through a critical exploration of some literature in moral philosophy. Chapter Five applies this definition of morality to two issues: whether law should enforce morality and what features the moral polity will possess.

Only the last chapter might count as a concrete discussion of social issues. But the other chapters are rich with topics significant for these issues: the truth value (if any) of evaluative statements; the distinction between physicalist and institutional language; the connections between *ought* and *is;* law as a premise for deducing *ought* statements; the role of purpose in legal systems; a formal account of morality; and so on. In a sense the issues typically found in value discussions *are* treated in these chapters, though at a level and in a manner which may not always be found in heated disputes among the "committed." This is an invitation to some cool thought.

There remains the task of drawing connections between the arguments of this book and the more immediate concerns any thoughtful
person will encounter in his daily life. Except possibly for the last chapter,
I have left these connections to the reader. But it is inconceivable that a
reading of this book will leave the reader unmoved on the issues of the
day. Whatever conclusions on academic freedom, objectivity, participation, and so on, are drawn from the discussion which follows, some shaft
of light, no matter how thin or weak, should be cast on these issues as
a result of reading this book. At the very least those discussions which
founder inconclusively on the observation, "Well, it's all finally just a
matter of opinion" will have been discredited. If just *that* deadening
moment in an argument, when values are hopelessly collapsed to opinion, is shattered by what follows, then the effort which went into this book
will have been worthwhile.

I have profited from the reading given the book in its manuscript
form by Professors Robert A. Dahl and Robert T. Holt. Both made
comments which saved me from errors, large and small. My thanks also
to my typist, Mrs. Diane Wallace, who, besides being an excellent typist,
has the distinction of being one of two people in the world who can read
my handwriting. (The other is not me—it is my wife.)

Fred M. Frohock
Madrid, 1973

CHAPTER ONE

METHODOLOGICAL NEUTRALITY

1. THE CASE FOR SCIENTIFIC NEUTRALITY

Whether the study of politics can be value-free, and even whether it ought to be, has vexed political scientists at least since Max Weber wrote at the beginning of this century. Weber argued strongly that social science can and ought to be conducted without evaluation. Though it is often forgotten in the heated debates over the argument itself, Weber thought he was providing an answer to an intolerable problem in his own historical circumstances. Many German scholars at the turn of this century were advocates of a semiauthoritarian government. This advocacy often intruded into the classroom. Weber was espousing a doctrine of neutrality in order, in part, to preserve the classroom as an area of free discussion.

The hope for nonpartisanship in teaching is not, however, the whole account of Weber's insistence on neutrality. The first occasion for his expression of value-free scholarship was his ascendancy to the editorial staff of a socioeconomic journal. In an article entitled (in the English-translation version) " 'Objectivity' in Social Science and Social Policy,"[1] Weber stated the intention of the journal to pursue only scientific research. This meant, for Weber, that the journal could not then *advocate* any values. Evaluations might still be a part of the journal's contributions. But these evaluations must be of the type which science can handle. Specifically, a scientific analysis for Weber can (1) determine the conceptual implications and internal consistency of value judgments, (2) uncover their possible factual consequences, (3) explore their premises, (4)

---

[1]Weber, in Edward A. Shils and Henry A. Finch, eds., *Max Weber on the Methodology of the Social Sciences* (Glencoe: The Free Press, 1949).

demonstrate the value assumptions of action and thought, and (5) reveal the optimal means-ends connections between certain goals and the methods of attaining these goals. What science cannot do, according to Weber, is establish the truth of values. Thus a journal devoted to science cannot take a final stand on what *ought* to be, although it may examine the logical and empirical status of *oughts* in the way described above.

Though there are many points of entry into Weber's case for value neutrality, four ideas drawn from the observations above will lead us into the tradition of value-free inquiry as effectively as any others. The first is the thought that the suspension of value judgments will present conditions for the effective exploration of ideas. John Stuart Mill, in *On Liberty,* argued for a marketplace of ideas, where the free exchange of thoughts in open debate will produce the best thoughts. Mill supported conditions of partisanship, advocacies freely pursued with an eye to discovering which ideas can withstand, and which will emerge from, the crosscurrents of debate. Weber's thesis on neutrality places the scholar as the observer of this free expression, permitting in the classroom the advocacy which he, the scholar, is denied under pain of constraining the free clash of ideas. The scholar, in short, is obligated to establish a laissez-faire system of learning, allowing the prices of ideas to be determined by the free flow of argument rather than through the restriction of intellectual activity. Such a mechanism, Weber thought, is necessary for effective education.

The second thought is that advocacy, like a shaft of light on Heisenberg's atoms, will change that which is the object of study, producing error in the scholar's research. The scientist may examine advocacy positions, as the teacher may discuss them, but he cannot take a stand himself without contaminating the subject. This is, like the first thought, a claim which is valid only in social science, for natural or nonhuman phenomena cannot express ideas or be contaminated with ideas. Contamination occurs in the entrance of the social scientist, through advocacy, into a social process. The social scientist who, for example, advocates his values to the citizen he is interviewing will risk swaying the citizen from his, the citizen's, own convictions, thus creating error in the interview (insofar as the interviewer is interested in getting at the respondent's attitudes independent of his own views). Similarly, a social anthropologist who stops infanticide in a primitive society will be carrying out his Western convictions, but at the sacrifice of accuracy in studying the primitive society.

Third, the affirmation of values will bias the scholar himself. Not only, as above, will advocacy in the classroom deny the conditions needed to recognize "better" ideas and thus thwart education, and in research cause distortion in social events, but a scholar who is part of an advocacy system will find himself unable to see the system clearly. Like the lawyer arguing for his client, he will tend to see the system from the point of view of his values. Weber's ideal scholar is like an ideal judge rather than a lawyer, detached and dispassionate, able to survey the proceedings from a neutral vantage point somewhere in the advocacy system. Scientific neutrality permits, according to Weber, the distance from experience which yields a cold and clear look at experience. Advocacy distorts this scrutiny by immersing the scholar's eye in one or another dimension of experience.

Fourth, and as a justification for excluding values from research, Weber accepts the thought that value judgments contain no truth content. It is helpful, in understanding this idea, to see statements in terms of the threefold classification system used by early logical positivists (a philosophical movement which has had much influence on the social sciences in this century). Briefly, logical positivists divided all statements into analytic, empirical, and value on the basis of a verificationist theory of meaning. By this is meant that, for positivists, the *meaning* of a statement is equivalent to how we *verify* it as true or false. Further, we have only two ways of verifying a statement: either in terms of the definitions of the words contained in the statement, or in terms of the correspondence of the statement to experience. As an example of the first type of verification, consider the following statement.

All bachelors are unmarried men.

This statement is true in terms of how we define the words "bachelor" and "unmarried men." It cannot be false as long as the subject of the statement, "bachelors" means "unmarried men," for the contrary of such a statement is merely a contradiction. Sometimes we say of such statements that the predicate ("are unmarried men") is contained in the subject ("All bachelors"). Such statements are *analytic* statements, often called tautologies, and exemplify the first kind of verification accepted by logical positivists.

An example of the second kind of verification is the following statement.

All bachelors are young men.

This statement is obviously not true by definition, for its contrary is not a contradiction. It *may* be true, or it may be false, but we do not know this until we investigate its correspondence to experience. It is an *empirical* statement. Such statements are often viewed as probabilistic, though at least one form of them (the example above) can be seen as universal descriptions which are falsified by a single counter instance, as in discovering one old bachelor.

Now contrast both statements with the following example.

All bachelors ought to get married.

Such a statement seems to be of a different logical order from the first two. While the first statement is a definitional assertion and the second is a claim about experience, this third statement is normative. According to the logical positivists, such a statement is not verifiable either analytically (for "ought to get married," or any part of this phrase, is not contained in a definition of "bachelors") nor empirically (for to say that something ought to be done is not to make a claim which can correspond *to* experience; it is to prescribe *for* experience, and this already entails that experience does not correspond to the ought—as bachelors must be unmarried for the prescription to marry to make sense). Since there is no other form of verification other than these two, at least for logical positivists, then normative statements cannot be said to be true or false. Further, if we link meaning to verification, as logical positivists do, then normative statements are, strictly speaking, meaningless.

A similar case can be made within positivism with respect to another kind of statement.

All bachelors are evil.

This statement does not prescribe anything directly. It is merely an evaluation. Yet it too seems markedly different from the first two kinds of statements. It is obviously not analytic, for "evil" is not part of the lexical meaning of "bachelor." Less obviously, though no less certain for logical positivists, the statement is not empirical. Being young, or old, is an attribute which a man has. But evil, according to positivists, is not an attribute of the world or those who inhabit it. It is a feeling or attitude on the part of the perceiving subject. Thus, to say that bachelors are evil is to express a feeling or state an attitude neither of which are true or false as they correspond to experience (as bachelors being young is verified by finding out whether they are or not) but only a way of revealing the disposition of whoever utters the statement.

The strength of the early positivists' separation of evaluative and factual terms rested on demonstrable distinctions between evaluative words and simple facts like colors. To say "X is red" seems clearly different than saying "X is good," for while the former is an attribute-statement the latter appears not to be. For example, a red house, a red car, and a red apple are all alike in their redness, suggesting that color is something an object "has." A good house, a good car, and a good apple, however, are all different in their goodness, suggesting that the predicate *good* is supervenient on facts and not just another fact about a thing. Further, that something is a fact is merely a matter of convention (or public validation), while at least one form of evaluation, *moral,* is not merely conventional. A dissent from factual reality is eccentricity, or worse, but dissenting from the moral consensus of one's society is usually regarded as a permissible move in moral discourse.

On the basis of this view of statements and how they are verified, logical positivists regarded all value statements (normative and evaluative) as meaningless on the grounds that they cannot be verified. For Weber, science is concerned with establishing truth and falsity. Since Weber worked with, in its essential characteristics, what later came to be called the positivist thesis on values, he was bound to exclude all value judgments from science on the grounds that such judgments make no truth claims. This he did. Notice, however, that both kinds of value statement, normative and evaluative, may be investigated in a scientific way. A normative statement may be verified as true or false for some state of affairs, as "All bachelors ought to get married in order to bring the crime rate down." In this case it has the status of an if-then proposition, and the connection between the *if* and the *then* can be established factually. (It is either true or not true that marriage is correlated positively with low crime rates.) Similarly, that people *feel* that bachelors are evil can be established factually. Also, if we stipulate defining criteria for evil, then whether bachelors fit under these criteria can be settled through scientific inquiry. What *cannot* be settled scientifically, and thus must be excluded from science, is the categorical truth of an ought (one not dependent on some state of affairs) or an evaluative-statement which is taken as asserting an attribute about experience.

Also, Weber was clear in admitting the role of values in the context of discovery or choice *prior* to doing science. How the scientist generates hypotheses or selects topics is, for Weber, a psychological and not a logical or empirical question. Values inform, and perhaps even define, this process. But the important matter is that science is subsequent to this process. After a "point of view" is accepted, a posture which includes even the first imperative of science that good explanations ought to be sought, then social inquiry can be value-free in focusing only on verifiable statements.

Finally, and as a supplement to the positivist thesis on values, Weber accepts the dictum normally associated with Hume that value statements cannot be logically derived from any set of premises not containing a value premise. The view of deduction implicit in this dictum is that nothing can be contained in the conclusion of a syllogism which isn't contained in one of the premises. An *ought* statement in a deduced conclusion must therefore entail an *ought* statement somewhere in the premises, or the deduction is invalid. Though Hume's logical separation between *is* and *ought* is aimed at normative statements, the same lack of entailment can be demonstrated for many evaluative statements. A word like *courage,* for example, is used both to describe and to commend, in that certain actions may be designated by the word and these actions are normally praised when the word is used to describe them. Yet the two dimensions of the word, the factual (descriptive) and evaluative (commendatory), may vary independent of each other. Two people may both commend with the use of the word courage and still disagree on what counts factually as courage. For one it may be courageous to accept any public challenge; for the other it may be precisely the highest form of courage to refuse any public challenge. In short, assenting to the factual dimension of a word like courageous does not require assenting to any particular evaluative dimension. No contradiction ensues in either case of the contraries (courageous = *s* accepting public challenge *vs.* courageous = *s* demurring from public challenges), as would be required if the relationship between facts and values were one of entailment. Consider, in contrast to the fact-value connection, the contradiction resulting from the contrary to an analytic statement, as "All bachelors are married men," where the relationship of subject ("bachelors") to predicate ("are married men") *is* one of entailment on the basis of how we define the words in the statement.

It follows from this view on values that not only must the social scientist remain neutral in doing research, he cannot as a scientist prescribe any final norms on the basis of his research. He may, as a citizen, be an advocate. But embracing final norms is as nonrational for him as for anyone else, for no facts, however comprehensive or detailed, will ever produce a statement on what ultimately ought to be done. Such statements are really not statements at all, but only emotive expressions; and in emotive expressions the scientist's expertise is no more important in an ultimate sense than the views of anyone else. The scientist may be more aware of such things as the conceptual underpinnings and empirical consequences of certain values. But, ultimately, each man must choose what ought to be done. No amount of knowledge will make that choice for him or compel him logically to make it. Policy, as basic prescriptions for society, is as much outside the domain of verified knowledge as are all other value judgments.

The case Weber makes for scientific neutrality, a case which has been influential in all important respects in contemporary social science, can be summed up as follows. Value judgments as advocacy positions are to be excluded from intellectual inquiry for four reasons. First, learning is facilitated when the scholar is not an advocate but a detached observer able to move in and out of ideas at will, and prepared to allow ideas to clash freely as a way of discovering their merit. Second, social events are altered when values are allowed to influence phenomena, thus creating error in social inquiry. Third, the social scientist is unable to perceive and understand social phenomena when he is a partisan, contributing further to the error suggested in the second reason. Fourth, value judgments do not in any case make truth claims. They are neither analytic nor empirical, nor deducible from facts. They are merely expressions of feeling or statements of attitude which can be verified only as if—then statements or provisional stipulations. Values thus properly affect science only as psychological considerations prior to the actual conduct of science. They are warranted neither (1) as advocacies in teaching or research, nor (2) as basic prescriptions based on scientific inquiry. The scientist is obligated to eschew values and remain neutral.

2. AN OPPOSING TRADITION

What exactly, it may be asked, is denied with the acceptance of the brief for scientific neutrality? Weber's thesis is opposed to all forms of what has been called value-cognitivism, a thesis which *does* claim truth content for value statements. It can take several forms. First, it may be claimed by a value-cognitivist that value statements are verifiable, like empirical statements, either on the grounds that values are attributes of experience like facts or that some state of affairs is sufficient to define a value term. Herbert Spencer's view of "fitness" as a kind of fact is an example of the former, while Jeremy Bentham's definition of "happiness" as the greatest good for the greatest number is often taken to be a version of the latter. Second, a value-cognitivist may claim that value statements are logically derivable from facts, as Jacques Maritain seems to maintain when he deduces natural law from facts about human nature. Third, values may be said to emerge from some factual process. All teleological theories, Aristotle's in particular, are versions of this view in accepting a normative outcome for natural processes. Fourth, value-cognitivism may rest on some state of mind, elite or mass. David Hume saw values as resting on "the enlightened opinion of mankind." John Stuart Mill defined pleasure as the "preferences felt by the majority of qualified judges." John Locke viewed certain values as self-evident truths. All three linked the truth of a value statement to preferences or attitudes of one sort or another. Fifth, a value-cognitivist may claim intuition as the method of verification for value statements. This fifth version may lodge values either in-the-nature-of-things (either as an attribute of empirical experience, as a principle transcending empirical experience, or as a part of a special kind of experience) or in a state of mind. G. E. Moore saw value as a special nonnatural property of things which is grasped intuitively. Intuition in Plato's philosophy is used to apprehend a principle, the Form of the Good, which transcends ordinary experiences. Leo Strauss locates the source of natural right in conditions where all artifice (or convention) is suspended. Jean-Jacques Rousseau regarded the laws of nature as "written in the depths of his (man's) heart by conscience and reason."

It is not necessary to explore each and every one of these forms of value-cognitivism to see that the tradition denied by Weber is rich and various. It is no exaggeration to view the greater part of the history of political theory as accepting value-cognitivism. From Plato through the utilitarians of the nineteenth century it was generally accepted that political theory is an extension of ethical theory in its concern for the good or just polity. Such a concern can be taken seriously only on the assumption that value statements *do* make truth claims, for otherwise the quest for ideal political arrangements has no more validity than a search for one's favorite ice cream. It is merely an exploration into taste. Certainly the great political theorists of the past did not, on the whole, view value statements as expressions only of feeling. There were exceptions, Hobbes' noncognitivism being a prominent one. But the political philosophy of Plato, Aristotle, Augustine, Aquinas, Locke, Rousseau, Mill, Bentham, and many more contains a normative dimension, consisting of statements on ideal political arrangements, on the assumption that value-cognitivism is sound.

It does not follow that a denial of truth content to value statements will entail an outright rejection of the larger part of the history of political theory. But at the very least the normative part of this tradition will have to be rethought. The adoption of Weber's view requires a judgment that much of political theory prior to the twentieth century is based on a mistake. It is hardly accidental that the denial of value-cognitivism in political inquiry in this century has also occasioned a crisis in the status of the history of political theory. If normative inquiry is impossible in the traditional way it has been done and explanation must rely on data in the here and now, then it is reasonable to dismiss the past as irrelevant to doing political theory in the present.

The stakes, in short, are high. Determining the validity, scope, and worthiness of the case for neutrality in social inquiry is no less than an inquiry into the nature and tradition of political theorizing itself.

3. IS NEUTRALITY DESIRABLE?

Weber's case for scientific neutrality is supported primarily in terms of the aims of science itself. It is offered as a way of insuring an accurate assessment of ideas and their consequences, as well as accuracy in collecting and interpreting data. Good science is value-free science, in that a value-free science will most completely realize the aim of science—explanation. However, given what we may have to discard by accepting Weber's thesis (the cognitive foundation for an inquiry into the good or just state) we may ask if scientific neutrality and its justification are desirable on terms other than those of science (leaving aside for the moment whether the thesis and its foundation are conducive even to good explanation).

One provision of the denial of value cognitivism normally considered desirable is moral freedom. If value statements have truth value, then moral judgments are true or false. This means not only that some moral claims are then ruled out because they are false, but also that one is then not free to choose any moral principle (anymore than one is free to choose any statement as a fact). One must entertain moral principles as hypotheses and ascertain their truth or falsity. Only "true" principles are sustainable. Consider what happens if someone dissents from a fact. He is considered eccentric, or ignorant, or worse. For example, a man who says X is not red when by all conventional standards it is, is either misusing language, color blind, or psychotic on colors. Now consider what happens when someone dissents from the moral consensus of his society. *This* dissent is still normally covered by moral discourse, as Antigone is thought to have acted morally when she buried her brother in opposition to the king.

If values are true or false, however, then we are not free to act contrary to the conventional results of settling on their truth or falsity. A moral conclusion, for example, which is deducible from a fact cannot be denied, for then we would be denying the fact. In Maritain's philosophy we are not free to accept or reject natural law once we accept certain facts about human nature. The natural law follows inexorably. If the king had been "right" morally on a cognitive version of value statements, then Antigone would have been "wrong," or acting falsely, by burying her brother. The *absence* of a necessary connection between facts and values, or the denial of truth content to value statements, is what provides for legitimate moral dissent. Otherwise, moral dissent must resemble factual dispute, which is never over facts but over whether something is a fact. It is an important feature of moral discourse that the acceptance of a moral principle still provides for freedom from conventional definitions of moral action.

It is possible to imagine moral principles *in* the conventions of society, not free of them. Value cognitivism provides for the possibility that what *ought* to be the case is identifiable with what *is* the case, or deducible from it. Thus a society may be arranged so that it is the source of moral direction. It is easy to see that no moral freedom is possible in such a society. Like factual judgments, a man is then bound to accept a given meaning for moral terms, that found in the conventions of his society. To be free to choose one's own moral principles requires that there be no entailment between facts and values. One is not, after all, free to choose or reject facts. To accept a necessary connection between facts and values is thus to transfer this constraint on facts over to evaluation.

A second provision of Weber's thesis which is ordinarily considered desirable is that it relies on knowledge as a publicly accessible commodity. Both types of statements which Weber accepts as verifiable, analytic and synthetic, depend for the establishment of their truth on methods which are explicit and available in principle to anyone. Contrast such a view of knowledge with Plato's insistence that the higher forms are accessible only to a few, and that the highest form, the Form of the Good, is apprehendible through an intuitive process which only a few can complete. These remarks are not meant to suggest that all versions of value-cognitivism rest on a private or elitist view of knowledge, for many do not —as in those theories which claim for values a deductive status from facts which anyone can acknowledge. However, *if* private or elitist views are regarded as offensive, then it is important to know that Weber's thesis does not share in the obnoxious idea that knowledge is a privileged property. All noncognitivist views accept the public quality of knowledge. Some cognitivist views find truth content in value statements by restricting the number of people who can have knowledge. Whatever Weber's deficiencies may be, *this* is not one of them.

Both these propositions, one of moral freedom and the other of publicly accessible knowledge, can be regarded as desirable aspects of scientific neutrality which are addenda to the purely scientific value of suspending values from describing and explaining. It is true that the primary justification for Weber's thesis will be in whether it is possible in the first place, and then whether it does what it purports to do, i.e., increase the accuracy of empirical inquiry, and finally whether empirical inquiry is itself defensible in the way Weber describes it. The remarks on desirability above contribute only to the last of these considerations, and the case against has yet to be heard. Still, it is worth something to know that scientific neutrality has some assumptions which may be justifiable in their own terms, apart from their contribution to "good" science.

4. IS NEUTRALITY POSSIBLE?

One of the strongest cases against Max Weber, and thus against neutrality in social science generally, is made by Leo Strauss. Strauss argues primarily against the possibility of carrying out the specifications on neutrality which Weber endorses, though he also views these specifications as undesirable. Strauss' case against the possibility of scientific neutrality consists of four claims. First, every social scientist must begin by distinguishing spurious and authentic instances of the phenomena he is studying, and this judgment is a value judgment. Second, the thesis of value neutrality is itself a value position with evaluative consequences. Anyone endorsing its validity is bound not to take seriously those who subscribe to value-cognitivism, thus biasing the study of all such thought when it is undertaken from a noncognitivist standpoint. Third, no nonevaluative language is available to study social events. Fourth, and as a point special to the study of politics, all political phenomena are purposive; and to study the purpose of political action is unavoidably to take an evaluative position.[2]

Before examining each of these claims separately, it should be noticed that Strauss' case does not rest with a simple demonstration that Weber's thesis is impossible. He takes the additional step of arguing that good social science must be evaluative, not neutral. It is possible, after all, to accept that good social science is achievable only through strict neutrality, but that the attainment of neutrality is a hopeless goal. Strauss accepts the hopelessness of attaining neutrality, but then denies a tragedy in this hopelessness. For Strauss, the very paradigm of good social science is a commitment to values, and to values of a very special sort (as we shall see in a moment).

4.1 The first claim made by Strauss, that every social scientist must make value judgments on the authenticity of the phenomena he is studying, seems undeniably true. Strauss points out that, in Weber's study of Protestantism, it was necessary for Weber to decide which of various religious movements in history are to "count" as Protestant, and which are to be considered spurious instances of the religion. We can find and multiply our own examples of authenticating judgments in social science. To study political parties, presidential power, religious sects, democracy, revolutions, and so on, will always require a prior identification of that which is to be studied.

Notice, however, that any random list of concepts, as in the examples above, will present different requirements for an identification. Some phenomena, like allegiance to a political party, are self-identifying. Whether an actor identifies with a political party, or even whether there exists a particular political party, is largely a matter for those involved in the event to decide. When authenticity is an issue, as when there may be competing claims for the "real" political party, or in deciding when a

---

[2]These claims can be found in two of Strauss' works, *Natural Right and History* (Chicago: University of Chicago Press, 1953), pp. 9–80, and *What is Political Philosophy* (Glencoe: The Free Press, 1959), pp. 9–55.

revolution has occurred, then the judgment of the social scientist is relevant. Even here, however, it does not follow necessarily that the social scientist will be judging *sui generis*. Social phenomena may occur in terms of well-defined rules which, in effect, make the judgment of authenticity virtually self-evident. A decision of what is to count, for example, as cloture in the Senate is not made by the social scientist, even if competing claims on cloture occur. The social scientist can only point to the Senate rules as the definitive say on authenticity. In social phenomena without such clear rules, as in the exercise of presidential power, there may be clear methodological rules not chosen by the social scientist doing the investigation which yet determine what is to count as the phenomenon in question. Any replication of a previous study will be bound by previous definitions of authenticity (even though they may result in new definitions eventually).

Let us assume, however, that neither social rules in a phenomenon nor methodological rules constrain the defining judgment of the social scientist. Seminal studies, as Weber's on Protestantism, or studies of concepts which have no clear rules nor have elicited agreement among social scientists on defining criteria, will be of this type. Studies of democracy, or revolutions, are often rule-less in these two senses also. Is the judgment on authenticity required of the social scientist a *value* judgment? It is certainly not a value judgment in the way in which Weber defines a value judgment, as an expression of favor or disfavor. One need not endorse a particular identification of a phenomenon in order to use the identification effectively. Suppose one accepts certain criteria, *a, b, c,* as an identifying mark for a religious sect. Is this equivalent to commending the criteria? It is a judgment of adequacy, for by accepting the criteria one has endorsed them as suitable for the investigation of the religious sect. But one has not endorsed anything beyond that. It is still possible to maintain, without a contradiction, that I accept criteria, *a, b, c,* as constituting an identification of a certain religion, but disapprove of the religion. If such a contrary were not possible, then only supporters of, say, fascism, could adequately study fascism. Even the identifying criteria may be endorsed only in the most provisional way, say as long as they are helpful in studying the phenomena, to be dismissed whenever they are no longer useful. Contrary to Strauss's first claim, it does not seem that an endorsement of a phenomenon is necessary in order to identify it.

4.2 The second of Strauss' claims, that the denial of objectively true norms then biases the study of those who do accept such norms, is an issue which depends upon what we mean by *bias*. Strauss specifically says that noncognitivists cannot "take seriously" those who claim truth content for value statements, which might count as a type of bias if it is unwarranted. Certainly if there *are* objectively true norms, then not taking claims for such norms seriously is a very clear case of bias. On the other hand, if value statements actually do not make truth claims, then one can hardly be blamed for treating lightly the assertions of those who claim they do. It is obvious that whether noncognitivism is biased in its treatment of cognitivist claims is to some extent a question of who is right, which is precisely the issue which separates the two positions. Thus how one settles the question depends in part on an answer to the prior question of whether one accepts the status of value statements assumed in the arguments of Weber or in the arguments of Strauss.

Perhaps a more general view of the issue Strauss poses, however, can be illuminated by considering whether the adoption of any theoretical position rules out the possibility of "taking seriously" an opposing position. Part of what must be considered is the phrase "take seriously."[3] Among the interpretations which might be given to it are (a) accept the validity of, (b) sympathize with, and (c) understand. It is obvious that if the phrase is to mean (a) then what Strauss says is true, though tautological as a criticism. It is precisely on the denial of truth value to value statements that noncognitivism is a distinct philosophy. Thus, as a philosophy, it cannot "take seriously," i.e., accept as a valid claim, cognitivism, though to say this is merely to repeat what the two terms, noncognitivism and cognitivism, mean. Nothing has been added to the meaning of the two terms by way of a criticism.

The more interesting issue, then, is whether the two other possible interpretations of "take seriously" can be held when the thesis being investigated is taken as invalid. Is it necessary to accept the validity of a claim in order to commend it or sympathize with it? The first of these interpretations seems to present a mixed case. Certainly the weight of one's convictions is toward disfavor in cases of invalidity, for an assertion of invalidity is normally an expression of disfavor. Something is said to be wrong with a thesis when it is said to be invalid. Yet we may find commendable things in an invalid argument, perhaps a certain substantive claim which, when presented differently, would be valid. In parliamentary debate, for example, a speaker may rule out of order, or invalid on the rules of debate, an argument with which he sympathizes in the most fervent way. The argument may be invalid on the terms of one discourse, parliamentary debate, while valid on the terms of some other discourse, say ethics. Even an argument invalid on all terms, or on fundamental terms (say one which is a logical contradiction) may yet have an ounce of attractiveness. One can commend the earnestness, for example, of an argument totally misconceived otherwise. But the point to make on this second interpretation of "take seriously" is that the mixed nature of

---

[3]The phrase is on p. 62 in Strauss, *Natural Right and History.*

the case is irrelevant to Strauss' claim. Whether a judgment of invalidity does or does not rule out a sympathetic view matters not to Weber's thesis on neutrality. The thesis concedes, indeed urges, the exclusion of commendations. So for Strauss to criticize Weber on this interpretation of "take seriously" would merely be to reinforce the most fundamental of Weber's claims, the very suspension of endorsement which distinguishes Weber's case.

This leaves us with the third interpretation of "take seriously," that of "understanding." Here the issue is important and revealing. Is the acceptance of validity a precondition for understanding an argument? At first glance this interpretation of the phrase in question seems to leave Strauss' claim in as weak a position as the first two interpretations. It is undeniable that in a wide range of cases understanding does not follow validity, but precedes it. One cannot, for example, determine the validity of a mathematical or logical proof unless one first understands it. Even the denial of the validity of value-cognitivism requires a prior understanding of the thesis. If Strauss' claim that noncognitivists cannot "take seriously" a cognitivist thesis means "understand," then the reverse seems true: that noncognitivists have to understand cognitivism before they can regard it as invalid.

On the other hand, there is also a sense in which validity and understanding go hand in hand. Some experiences, for example marriages, may require an acceptance of validity in order to be the experiences that they are. Does a trial marriage amount to the same experience as a marriage? On the third interpretation of Strauss' key phrase, it might be said that as long as the relationship between two people is a "testing" one, or provisional in any sense, that the experience of marriage has not been realized. The same thing may be said of all experiences where an acceptance of the validity of an arrangement is necessary to experience the arrangement. Religious vows, prison terms, generally any social arrangement with a definitive provision, will be different without the definitive provision. Now it is true that one can "understand" experiences like marriage without being married. But there is also a sense in which having an experience leads to an understanding not accessible from merely observing the experience. If one allows that experience is a source of knowledge, a claim difficult to deny, then it is inescapable that one understands an experience differently in doing it than in not doing it. When the condition for having an experience is the acceptance of its validity, then some form of understanding does depend upon the acceptance of validity.

It should be evident that there are two dimensions to this interpretation of Strauss' claim. The first is a recognition of a difference between experience which is dependent on the acceptance of validity, and that which is not. Marriage has been suggested as one example of the former. Any noncommittal experience, say driving a car, can exemplify the latter. The second is an acceptance of a distinction between detached understanding (from the stance of an observer) and involved understanding (from the stance of a participant). For Strauss' claim on understanding to make sense, he must combine these two dimensions in the following way. Only a kind of experience is fugitive to Weber's noncognitivism, that which entails a validity acceptance to be what it is; and the only understanding which escapes Weber's framework is that which is unique to participation in experience as opposed to observation of experience.

Taken in this way, Strauss' claim on understanding makes sense. It is reasonable to accept that a certain quality of experience is missing when life is studied from a detached perspective. And certainly when experience depends for its authenticity on an acceptance of validity, then a neutral stance is unable to understand this experience. This interpretation of Strauss also reveals some of the major differences in methods of inquiry between two important schools of thought. For Weber, as we have seen, social events are studied most accurately from a dispassionate perspective, one which is removed from the social scene by virtue of its dispassionateness. Strauss, on the other hand, is sympathetic to a participant stance, where the social theorist is immersed in that experience he is explaining. In short, the dispute between Weber and Strauss over the possibility of a value-free social science very quickly turns into a dispute over detached *vs.* participant social analysis, the former established by a suspension of endorsement and the latter required by the acceptance of endorsement.

4.3 The third of Strauss' claims against Weber, that there is no such thing as a nonevaluative language for the social scientist to use as a vehicle for neutrality, may be the most important point on which the Weber-Strauss dispute turns. Accepting Weber's version of a value-judgment as an expression of favor or disfavor (or, as interpreted here, an endorsement), then it is helpful to see such expressions in terms of a tripartite arrangement of language. At one level are what might be called first-order judgments, where the value judgment is the primary function of the proposition. Value judgments containing the words *good, ought,* and *right* comprise this class. Another class of value judgments may be called second-order, these containing words which are both descriptive and evaluative. *Courageous, diligent, communist,* are some examples of such words. A third class of value judgments, to be called third-order judgments, will contain none of the evaluative words marking off the first two classes of judgments, but will function as evaluations *in use.* "Jane Smith is a student" is nonevaluative linguistically, but is an evaluation when used as a response to the query: "I need a seasoned professional for this job. How about Jane Smith?" All three orders of judgment are, or may be, evaluations. But, as language, the first is a statement which primarily evaluates, the second combines description and evaluation, the third is a description which can always function as an evaluation.

Using this arrangement of language, it is clear that the issue of value neutrality will differ depending upon which order of evaluation is at issue. For Weber, value neutrality seems to mean a suspension of first-order evaluations, especially those containing the word *ought*. This is easy enough to visualize, for it takes no effort to see description and explanation occurring without *ought* judgments (and thus without endorsements). But to someone of Strauss' persuasions, this would be a neutralization of only the tip of the evaluative matrix. One may still suspend first-order evaluations while evaluating in second- or third-order terms. Strauss' denial of Weber's case for neutrality, given the reasonable possibility of excluding first-order evaluations from social science, must rest on a demonstration that one or both of these latter orders of evaluation are necessary in any language of social inquiry.

Since the second- and third-order classes of judgments extend to all language use, then it is undeniable that the language of both orders of value judgment must be part of social inquiry. But whether evaluation is necessarily a part of such language, and what kind of evaluation goes on in such language, is not clear. Let's examine second-order judgments first. It is commonly accepted that when we say of someone that he is, say, diligent, we are both describing and evaluating the person. Certain facts, say spending long hours on a job, staying with a problem until a solution is found, not being distractable when at work, and so on, will ordinarily count as a description of diligence. They can be stated in the form of factual propositions, as in statements that a certain person works 12 hours a day. But, also, the term "diligence" is used to commend, for to say of someone that he is diligent is ordinarily to pay a compliment, to praise. Similarly, when we say of someone that he is a fascist, we are using a term which has a descriptive component *and* an evaluative component. We describe, but (in this case) we also condemn.

The thing to notice about this duality of purpose in second-order judgments is that there does not ordinarily seem to be a necessary connection between the factual and evaluative components of such terms. (Whether there is a necessary connection in some circumstances will be explored later.) The descriptive component of fascism, for example, has remained substantially the same from the 1930s to the present time. Yet in Germany in the 1930s the term would have ordinarily been used to praise. Today it is used to condemn. The evaluative component has changed independent of the factual component. It should also be noticed that, as pointed out earlier, assenting to the factual component of a second-order term does not seem always to entail an assent to the evaluative component. One can accept all of the factual statements specifying a lexical definition of courage, and still condemn the actions described by the definition without involving oneself in a contradiction. It should be stressed that this is a logical point only. If "courage" is applied in ordinary conversation it is reasonably assumed to be an item of praise. But it is logically possible to say of someone that he is courageous, though I loathe and despise courage.

The independence, or lack of entailment, between the factual and evaluative components of second-order terms means that the social scientist using such terms need not subscribe to the evaluations to use the terms as descriptions. In effect, it becomes possible to separate the evaluations of the social theorist from the evaluations of his language. A social scientist, in using a second-order term like "fascist," may be either praising or condemning, or neither. The term itself, given the absence of entailment between its descriptive and evaluative components, does not require any form of endorsement, or even endorsement itself. Thus Weber's neutrality, as a suspension of endorsement, may be preserved even in the face of second-order evaluative terms.

With such victories, however, Weber may not have to worry about defeats. What is conceded with this preservation of neutrality is the possibility that all of social science may be evaluative while the social scientist is neutral. For this reason social scientists often try to neutralize the evaluative overtones of their language as well as insure that they, as social scientists, abstain from endorsements. It means little, after all, if a social theorist withholds an evaluation while his social theory contains words which function as evaluations. Democracy, for example, is a word with an evaluative component reflecting centuries of pejorative use in practical politics. To use it theoretically today in a nonevaluative explanation requires that the word be given a stipulative definition by the social scientist which neutralizes its evaluative content.

It is not certain, however, if this neutralization can be carried out with unqualified success. Stipulating new meanings for old words still leaves a connection between the stipulation and the lexical definitions; for one cannot say that a word in the language will now mean $X, Y, Z,$ without also, whenever the stipulation is used, implicitly referring to the word which has been given a new meaning. Also, stipulating new meanings for second-order terms may produce only new second-order terms. Seymour Lipset, for example, has defined democracy in a complex society as "a political system which supplies regular constitutional opportunities for changing the government officials, and a social mechanism which permits the largest possible part of the population to influence major decisions by choosing among contenders for political office."[4] Though nowhere do we find clearly second-order evaluations like "courage" and "fascist" in this definition, neither do we find strict third-order type factual terms either. Terms like "constitutional," "opportunities," "choosing" will ordinarily carry some commendatory force.

Suppose, however, that social science can be conducted without either first-order or second-order evaluative terms. Say the language of social inquiry is approximate in its evaluate force to straightforward physicalist language, where the facts are included and nothing more. Will social inquiry *then* be value-free? Not necessarily. Any factual proposition may function as an evaluation if the circumstances are right. Think, to make this point clear, of the most nonevaluative description possible, say the statement "He is 5' 10" tall." This statement is a perfectly straightforward description of physical attributes and, on the surface, seems as neutral as any statement can possibly be. Now imagine the statement uttered in response to the following statements: "A height of 5' 11" is the minimum required for entrance to the service academy. How tall is that applicant over there?" If it is so easy to imagine physicalist descriptions functioning as evaluations in suitable contents, then how much easier it is to see social language, filled with the terms of human interactions, as evaluations in one context or another. The point is not that social theory is necessarily evaluative, for one can as easily construct contexts in which third-order statements function nonevaluatively. The point is rather that any assertion of social science, no matter how nonevaluative it is in terms of its language, may be evaluative in the right circumstances.

Weber's neutrality thesis is damaged by these remarks in two ways. First, the suspension of *ought* judgments stressed so strongly by Weber is irrelevant to the evaluative qualities of language in terms of second-order words. Second, the suspension of second-order evaluations is by no means a clearly successful enterprise. Whether stipulative definitions can totally filter out evaluative qualities is problematic. The third-order type of evaluation is not covered by Weber's thesis. Weber is not concerned with the use to which social science is put, only with the neutrality of social inquiry. It is important to remember, however, that neutrality in inquiry (if it somehow can be achieved) is consistent with an evaluative function for explanations when they are located in suitable social contexts. And it is also equally important that we see the other side of the coin, which is that third-order propositions can function nonevaluatively in certain contexts as well. It follows that social science may always be

---

[4]Lipset, *Political Man: The Social Bases of Politics* (New York: Anchor Books, 1963), p. 27.

evaluative, no matter how strictly the social scientist maintains his neutrality, but social science is not necessarily evaluative either (as Strauss maintains) as long as third-order propositions can function as a nonevaluative language.

4.4 The last of Strauss' claims, that the notion of *purpose* must dictate an evaluative quality for social inquiry, is an argument aimed solely at political theorists. Strauss argues that all political action has an end and this end is evaluative.

> All political action is then guided by some thought of better or worse. But thought of better or worse implies thought of the good. . . .

> All political action has then in itself a directedness towards knowledge of the good: of the good life, or of the good society. For the good society is the complete political good.[5]

Though there is much on which we might want to demur in what the "complete political good" suggests, the idea of political action as goal-directed and evaluative in choosing and securing goals is one we might all accept. Certainly Weber recognizes that to be an agent engaged in action is to have purposes and to evaluate. The neutrality of social science depends on taking these goals and evaluations as facts to be explained. Strauss, however, denies that they can be taken as facts. The presence of purpose in political action entails, for Strauss, an evaluation by the political theorist.

> There is a variety of regimes. Each regime raises a claim, explicitly or implicitly, which extends beyond the boundaries of any given society. These claims conflict, therefore, with each other. There is a variety of conflicting regimes. Thus the regimes themselves, and not any preoccupation of mere bystanders, *force us* to wonder which of the given conflicting regimes is better, and ultimately, which regime is the best regime.[6] (Italics added.)

Are we forced into evaluation by the fact of purpose, as Strauss asserts? It does not seem so. We may wonder about the values someone possesses, a wonderment that may lead us into a critical evaluation of these values and their alternatives. But *may* and not *must* is surely the operative word here. Describing a purpose does not entail evaluating that purpose (though our descriptions, as we have seen, may carry their own evaluations, which are themselves not necessarily related to the purpose being described). The statement "John Smith intends to have dinner at

---

[5]Strauss, *What is Political Philosophy,* p. 10.
[6]Strauss, *What is Political Philosophy,* p. 34.

6:00 P.M." may be evaluative in some contexts, but can function nonevaluatively; and even when it *is* an evaluation it need not be an evaluation of John Smith's intentions. As an answer to the question, "When is John Smith having dinner?," the statement is a routine fact. To the proposition and query, "All prisoners will have dinner at 5:00 P.M. When does prisoner John Smith think he's going to eat?," the statement is an evaluative insight into Smith's level of subordination or recalcitrance. But Smith's intentions still have not been evaluated, as they are with first-order judgments of good and bad goals for prisons and prisoners.

The descriptive language of politics seems equally flexible when it comes to handling purposes. Recognizing the evaluative function of political action does not always require taking a position on the different values contained in this function. Were this degree of detachment not possible the very act of evaluating would be jeopardized, for even to state that politics reconciles conflicting purposes is to advance a definition which occasions, but is not itself, the evaluations Strauss requires. If the language of politics were only evaluative, then these evaluations represented by judgments of the just or unjust state would be impossible. Only as the term "state" is *not* evaluative is it possible to assign evaluations of justice to it without either a contradiction or a tautology.

5. THE ISSUES STATED

The discussion so far has focused primarily on two figures in political thought, Max Weber and Leo Strauss. It is easy to see, however, how the differences between these two theorists extend to the general issues raised by any case for neutrality in social inquiry. They can be summarized as follows.

1. Is *ought* separable from *is?* Weber's case depends upon a logical distinction between normative and empirical statements in order to suspend *oughts* from social inquiry. If some entailment can be demonstrated between the two, then the possibility of neutrality in social inquiry is commensurately limited.

2. Even allowing for an *ought-is* distinction, is advocacy contained in second-order evaluations? Though this issue is more suitably explored in terms of particular theories and the language contained in them, the same lack of entailment between the evaluative and descriptive dimensions of second-order terms is necessary for Weber's neutrality thesis. If entailment can be demonstrated, then the general substance of Weber's case collapses.

3. What effect does detachment (Weber) *vs.* partisanship (Strauss) have on the study of social events? This issue is more complicated than

can be easily discussed here. However, the discussion in the text suggests that one root to the neutrality controversy is what kind of social science one is prepared to accept as more authentic: observation or involvement. Adopting one or the other of these stances for understanding and explaining social phenomena will lead reasonably to either a Weberian or Straussian position on values in social inquiry.

4. Even granting the lack of entailment between facts and values, to what extent does the evaluative function of social science *in use* constrain the scope of neutrality? Here it is even more important to understand that this is an empirical question resolvable only through investigation of the evaluative functions (third-order) of explanations in social theory, though it is also important to see the distinctions which mark this empirical question off from the more conceptual concerns of first- and second-order evaluations.

Like most first chapter discussions, the excursions here suggest more than they resolve. Though there is no guarantee that later discussions will be more conclusive, at least we can be clearer now about the deeper considerations involved in the issue of values in social inquiry. Of first importance is the obviously different views on language held by neutrality advocates and those denying neutrality. To argue neutrality requires a view of language which permits considerable autonomy for the user, in separating his evaluations from his descriptions and in detaching himself from the language of participant action. The opponent of neutrality, on the other hand, will deny this autonomy. For him, language compels, moves the user inexorably to certain evaluations and points of view.

To these two views of language we must now turn in our exploration into evaluation and neutrality.

FOR FURTHER READING

Austin, J. W. *How to Do Things With Words.* Edited by J. O. Urmson. London: The Clarendon Press, 1962.

Ayer, A. J. *Language, Truth and Logic.* New York: Dover Publications, Inc., 1946.

Brecht, Arnold. *Political Theory.* Princeton, N.J.: Princeton University Press, 1959.

Gellner, Ernest. *Words and Things.* Baltimore: Penguin Books Inc., 1968.

MacIntyre, Alasdair. *A Short History of Ethics.* New York: The Macmillan Company, 1966.

Mehta, Ved. *Fly and the Fly-Bottle.* Baltimore: Penguin Books Inc., 1965.

Oppenheim, Felix. *Moral Principles in Political Philosophy.* New York: Random House, Inc., 1968.

Strauss, Leo. *Natural Right and History.* Chicago: The University of Chicago Press, 1953.

_____. *What is Political Philosophy*. Glencoe: The Free Press, 1959.

Urmson, J. O. *Philosophical Analysis*. Oxford: The Clarendon Press, 1956.

_____. *The Emotive Theory of Ethics*. New York: Oxford University Press, Inc., 1968.

Warnock, Mary. *Ethics Since 1900*. Oxford: Oxford University Press, Inc., 1966.

Weber, Max. *The Methodology of the Social Sciences*. Glencoe: The Free Press, 1949.

Wilson, John. *Language and the Pursuit of Truth*. Cambridge: Cambridge University Press, 1967.

CHAPTER TWO

THE NEW NATURALISM

1. ON DERIVING OUGHT FROM IS

One of the beliefs vital to positivist social science has been the thesis that *ought* cannot be derived from *is*. Stated formally, it consists of the claim that no statement containing an *ought* can be deduced from any set of premises which do not contain an *ought*. The claim rests on a fundamental truth of logic, that nothing can be contained in the conclusion of a syllogism that is not present somewhere in the premises. The legacy of the thesis is usually traced to Hume. In a famous passage in the *Treatise on Human Nature,* Hume observed that

> I cannot forbear adding to these reasonings an observation which may perhaps be found of some importance. In every system of morality which I have hitherto met with I have always remarked that the author proceeds for some time in the ordinary way of reasoning, and establishes the being of a God, or makes observations concerning human affairs; when of a sudden I am surprised to find, that instead of the usual copulations of propositions, *is* and *is not,* I meet with no proposition that is not connected with an *ought,* or an *ought not.* This change is imperceptible; but is, however, of the last consequence. For as this *ought* or *ought not* expresses some new relation or affirmation, it is necessary that it should be observed and explained; and at the same time that a reason should be given for what seems altogether inconceivable, how this new relation can be a deduction from others that are entirely different from it.[1]

The importance of this thesis in modern social science is impossible to exaggerate. Accepted as a truth beyond the pale of criticism it has

[1] *Treatise,* Book III, Part 1, Section i.

23

functioned as an important justification for scientific neutrality. The justification rests on the reasonable proposition that scientists are concerned with statements of fact; and if no set of factual statements, no matter how comprehensive, will serve to deduce a statement on what ought to be done, then *ought* statements would not seem to be the concern of scientists.

Yet one must be careful not to misunderstand the *is-ought* disjunction even when its truth is conceded. Nowhere in the thesis is it written that facts and values are unrelated to one another in all ways. It is merely that they are not *deductively* connected. Thus facts may have an effect upon oughts in a variety of ways even if they cannot function as premises for the deduction of *oughts*. Weber, as we have seen, was not ignorant of these possibilities, allowing that facts can help settle the feasibilities of *oughts* and even their desirability. The value of an end, for example, is in part a matter of its acquisition costs and its consequences. But such calculations are parasitic on the truth of the logical separation between *ought* and *is*. If values *can* be deduced from facts, then a direct connection obtains between science and what ought to be done which makes any other calculation on facts and values peripheral. Thus the question generally taken for granted in social science is the one rich with implications: Is the logical distinction between *ought* and *is* valid?

1.1. John Searle has offered a counterexample to Hume's generally accepted thesis which claims the deduction of an *ought* from premises not containing an *ought*.[2] The deduction occurs in terms of the following series of statements.

1. Jones uttered the words "I hereby promise to pay you, Smith, five dollars."
2. Jones promised to pay Smith five dollars.
3. Jones placed himself under (undertook) an obligation to pay Smith five dollars.
4. Jones is under an obligation to pay Smith five dollars.
5. Jones ought to pay Smith five dollars.

Searle argues that each statement and its successor are more than contingently related, and the additional statements needed to make the relationships one of entailment are not evaluative statements, or anything like evaluative statements. The most important relationship, however, is that between statement five and its predecessors; for if it is a valid deduction from the four prior statements, and these statements are factual (or

[2]Searle, "How to Derive 'Ought' from 'Is,' " in W. D. Hudson, ed., *The Is-Ought Question* (New York: St. Martin's Press, Inc., 1969), pp. 120–34.

descriptive) without being evaluative, then an *ought* has been deduced from an *is.* And Hume's thesis, if not wrong, is at least restricted in its scope.

The first thing to inspect in assessing Searle's derivation is the "additional statements" which are needed to make the derivation a deduction. They are as follows:

Between 1 and 2:
  1a. Under certain conditions C anyone who utters the words (sentence) "I hereby promise to pay you, Smith, five dollars" promises to pay Smith five dollars.
  1b. Conditions C obtain.
Between 2 and 3:
  2a. All promises are acts of placing oneself under (undertaking) an obligation to do the thing promised.
Between 3 and 4:
  3a. Other things are equal.
  3b. All those who place themselves under an obligation are, other things being equal, under an obligation.
Between 4 and 5:
  4a. Other things are equal.
  4b. Other things being equal, one ought to do what one is under an obligation to do.

Two immediate issues arise when Searle's derivation is thus fleshed out. First, are the premises (primary and additional statements) of the deduction merely factual and not evaluative? Second, do the premises permit the deduction of the conclusion, given that they are nonevaluative? To these two issues may be added a third, more general than the first two: How is the derivation possible in the face of logical rules prohibiting the deduction of anything in a conclusion not somewhere contained in the premises?

1.2. The first objection to Searle's derivation can be a restatement of the rules of logic indicated above. Since a deduced conclusion cannot contain anything not present in the premises, this objection may run, then Searle's premises *must* contain an evaluation.[3] Though this objection begs the question, it does suggest the need for further explanation on how the derivation is possible.

Searle's derivation depends upon a distinction between two kinds of "fact." One is institutional, the other not. An institutional fact is any

---

[3]This objection is cited by Searle, "How to Derive 'Ought' from 'Is.' "

state of affairs which entails some institution in order to be what it is. For example, the proposition "Senator Jones voted for open housing last week" is a description of Senator Jones' actions, and certainly not equivalent to saying that it is *good* that Senator Jones voted the way he did or that Senator Jones *ought* to vote even more frequently for open housing. But it is a description which depends upon the institution of the Senate, and is different from those descriptions of Senator Jones (and what he does) which do not depend upon institutions. To say, for example, "Jones is six feet tall," or "Jones has black hair," or "Jones weighs 180 pounds," is to describe in a noninstitutional way. Such statements are what have been called "brute" facts, for they describe states of affairs which are not reliant for their existence on institutions.[4]

It is undeniable that all descriptive statements, by virtue of being statements, are reliant on rules. One type of rule is that by which a society settles on what counts as a description, as even the "brute" fact of Jones being 55 years old will suggest different things depending on whether convention dictates that years be counted from conception or from birth. Another type of rule is linguistic, including those rules which provide criteria for well-formed sentences. Such rules (and many others) provide no basis for distinguishing institutional and noninstitutional facts. They may even, given the slippery use of the word "institution," count as institutions of sorts in being systems of rules. So it is reasonable to ask, what exactly is an "institution" in the phrase "institutional fact"?

We may, with Searle, distinguish between rules which regulate an activity, as etiquette rules regulate eating, and constitutive rules, which regulate *and* define an activity, as chess rules state what it is to play chess. One can eat without following the rules of etiquette. But one cannot play chess without following the rules of chess. An institutional fact is a state of affairs which, as in the example of chess, is logically dependent on a set of rules for its existence. Thus an "institution" here means a set of constitutive rules. Hitting a home run, for example, is an action which exists only within the institution of baseball, an activity comprised of constitutive rules. Swinging a piece of wood, striking a spherical object hard enough to propel it over a distant fence, etc., is a "brute" or—in the language of the first chapter—physicalist fact. It is a state of affairs which exists independent of rules. Now, again, it is undeniable that certain rules will govern the statements describing physicalist actions, as what is to count as wood, spherical, etc., will depend upon certain conventions, perhaps, in this case, geometrical systems, found in society. But the

----

[4]G. E. M. Anscombe, "On Brute Facts," *Analysis,* 18 (1958).

physical action occurs independent of the systems of rules, whatever they are. It is this which makes the statements describing such actions statements of "brute" or physicalist fact. Hitting a home run, however, is an action which can occur only in terms of an institution. It is this logical dependence of the action on the rules which makes statements describing such actions statements of institutional fact. In one of Searle's examples, that a man has a piece of paper with green ink on it is a brute fact. That he has five dollars is an institutional fact.

It is clear that no deduction of an *ought* is possible from premises which are stated in physicalist language. From the fact of Jones being 55 years old, or six feet tall, or prone to hardening of the arteries, nothing seems to follow in the way of an *ought*. One can use such facts to support an *ought,* as Weber pointed out. For example, the fact that Jones' arteries are hardening may be a reason for Jones to exercise. He really ought to exercise, we might feel inclined to say. But the *ought* must be carefully prepared for by an evaluative premise, that hardening of the arteries is bad news because it leads to early deaths, which are also bad. Without the evaluative premises no *ought* follows. (Sometimes, as is common with Weber, the evaluative premise is stated as a goal with the directive *ought* then seen as a means to that goal, as exercise is good in that it leads to good health, etc.) Nor, it should be added, will all institutional facts function as premises for the derivation of an *ought*. The fact that Jones voted for open housing leads nowhere evaluatively. It may be a good or bad action, something Jones ought or ought not to have done, depending entirely on the introduction of some evaluative principle. The evaluative principle is not contained within the institutional fact *as* an evaluation.

Some institutional facts, however, do seem to function as premises for the derivation of *oughts,* or so Searle claims. To describe someone as promising seems to lead to the thought that he ought to do what he promises. The reason for this is not, according to Searle, because there is some hidden evaluative premise in a description of promising. We are still stating a fact, that Jones promised to pay Smith five dollars, but it is a fact which exists only in terms of the institution of promise-keeping; and it is the rules of this institution, not any evaluative premise (as an endorsement within the derivation), which makes the deduction of an *ought* possible. Promising, like chess, is a system of constitutive rules. The utterance of certain words is a promise only in terms of these rules, which in the case of promising are summed up simply enough with the undertaking of an obligation. Thus to describe someone as promising requires that we are describing him as taking on an obligation, which then seems tautologous with the proposition that he ought to keep the obligation.

The description, in short, is impossible without the statement of the obligation, though it is not also necessary to endorse the activity of promising in order to describe it.

To the question, how is the derivation possible, the answer then is this. Positivist social scientists like Weber fail to distinguish between two quite different kinds of facts, physicalist and institutional. The thesis which holds to a logical separation between *is* and *ought* rests on *is* being defined in purely physicalist terms. When institutional facts are introduced, and when these institutional facts exist within systems of constitutive rules which state obligations, commitments, and responsibilities, then we can logically derive *ought* from *is*.

There still remains the question from logic. How can an evaluative conclusion be deduced from premises not containing an evaluation? There are three possible answers to this. First, it might be maintained that the evaluation stated in the conclusion is present in the premises, but not as an endorsement. It is, in the premises, that which is described, and, in the conclusion, that which binds the person described. On this answer the derived *ought* commits only Jones, the man who promised; and while *ought* has been derived from *is,* the concluding *ought* is a statement on Jones' obligation which in no way commits the person doing the describing and deriving. Thus the premise is descriptive, stating an obligation for Jones, and the conclusion is descriptive also, stating an obligation for Jones. Second, it might be said that the use of certain descriptive terms, like promising, commits one *as user* to the *oughts* constituting the activity the terms define. To say, on this interpretation, that one is describing someone as promising is to commit oneself to the proposition, all other things being equal, that the one described ought to keep his promises. The evaluation, in this case, is present in the description and is carried forward to the conclusion, and it binds observer and participant (whoever describes Jones and Jones). Third, it might be said that the evaluation contained in the conclusion of the deduction is in the premises as a fact, the action described, and then is transformed into a binding ought in the course of the deduction; that, in effect, the deduction restates the fact that an obligation has been undertaken, but in the form of a prescription binding on both the observer and participant.

The third explanation of how the deduction is possible extends our commonplace assumptions on what deductions do. But this is not such a novel move. It is also commonly assumed that analytic statements add nothing in the way of information, since (as we have seen) the predicate of such a statement is contained in the subject. But when we inspect specific analytic statements we discover otherwise. To say, for example, that "A puppy is a young dog" is to utter an analytic statement. Yet it is an obviously informative proposition, especially for one unfamiliar with the meaning of the subject.[5] The conventional wisdom on deductive proofs may be similarly deficient. To say that a deduced conclusion merely restates what is contained in the premises (much as the predicate of an analytic statement restates what is in the subject) is to say nothing about how the deduction affects that which is extracted and concluded. An evaluation in the form of a fact, as an action described, may become a prescription (an *ought*) as the consequence of a deduction. The institutional fact of a promise *becomes* prescriptive when we state the constitutive rule of obligation as the logical conclusion of a deduction from this fact. This third explanation obviously calls into question the very rule of logic which blithely denies the logical derivation of *ought* from *is*.

It is even more important to see, however, that all three explanations for the deduction raise questions about how an evaluation differs from a description. The proposition "Jones promised to pay Smith five dollars" is obviously a description. Yet, like a prism turning in sunlight, it seems also to become an evaluation with a variety of forms and possibilities. The most instructive way to examine such a proposition is to see it in terms of Searle's derivation, carefully exploring where Searle succeeds and fails, and what the derivation and the propositions comprising its premises mean for the conduct of social science.

2. SOME OBJECTIONS

The first objection to Searle's derivation can be directed at the *ceteris paribus* clauses. What is it, one might ask, for all other things to be equal? A *ceteris paribus* clause is a common feature of both explanatory theories and moral reasoning. In the former, it generally functions as a statement establishing the absence of invalidating conditions in a causal relationship between two or more events. We often, in an offhand way, say that something causes something else "all other things being equal." This casual deference to the phrase is commonly stated more formally in empirical science, as *A* causes *B* when *C*. It is often taken to be the mark of an advanced science that the *C* can be specified with some precision and detail, or that we know in advance not only what the "all other things" are that must be equal, but what it is for them to be equal for particular conditions. Most versions of moral reasoning rely on a *ceteris paribus* clause to establish obligation, the clause functioning as a statement on defeating conditions or exceptions to moral prescription. For example, the prescription enjoining killing is normally set aside when

[5]On this point see Robert Holmes, "The Case Against Ethical Naturalism," *Mind*, LXXIII (April 1964), pp. 291–95.

self-defense is demonstrated. A demonstration of self-defense is a demonstration of relevant dissimilarity, or that all other things are *not* equal.

Searle relies on *ceteris paribus* clauses in moving from statement 3 (Jones placed himself under (undertook) an obligation to pay Smith five dollars) to statement 4 (Jones is under an obligation to pay Smith five dollars), and in moving from statement 4 to statement 5 (Jones ought to pay Smith five dollars). It is easy to see why the *ceteris paribus* clauses are needed. If it turns out that Jones' wife has squandered his entire fortune during the time that he is out making promises, to the point where paying Smith five dollars will prevent him, Jones, from feeding his children adequately, then we normally want to say that Jones may have placed himself under an obligation but he is not in fact under an obligation because of these extenuating circumstances. Or if it turns out that Jones' wife is sufficiently frugal so that Jones has the money to pay Smith, but it is discovered that if Smith gets the five dollars back he will use it to buy a cheap handgun to kill his own wife, a purchase he cannot make without the return of the five dollars, then we may want to say that Jones' obligation is vitiated by Smith's deranged attitude. Jones ought not to pay Smith the five dollars (in such a case) even though normally the obligation requires that he ought to pay.

In both examples circumstances prevent a move from one statement to its successor. The *ceteris paribus* clauses are statements to the effect that circumstances like these, those which defeat or set aside the obligation or the concluding *ought,* do not obtain. Searle views these *ceteris paribus* clauses as descriptive statements, propositions to the effect that all other things are equal. Yet while the statement of each *ceteris paribus* clause may be descriptive, perhaps a merely negative description that no extenuating circumstances exist, it is instructive to see how circumstances become extenuating in the first place. Suppose it were claimed that, regardless of whether Jones had funds to feed his children, he still is obligated to pay Smith that five dollars. Or that Jones ought to pay Smith the money regardless of how Smith intends to use it. What kind of an argument might one marshall against such claims (assuming that one were disposed to argue against them)? It is obvious that the claims are not illogical. Uttering them involves no contradiction. They are coherent claims based on an evaluative premise different from the one which accepts the circumstances as extenuating. To argue against them it is necessary to argue the superiority of one evaluative principle over another. If this is so, then it follows that what is to count as extenuating circumstances is a question of what evaluative principle one adopts. The *ceteris paribus* clauses are descriptive statements, but they rest on a prior evaluative principle which distinguishes some conditions as relevant reasons for defeating an *ought* from all other conditions which do not. Thus, this objection may conclude, Searle's derivation contains an implicit evaluation in the premises, that which informs the *ceteris paribus* clauses and identifies the "all other things" which must be equal for the *ought* to be deduced.[6]

Two strategies seem open to Searle in countering this objection. One he has adopted outright in a later version of the derivation. It consists of moving the *ceteris paribus* clauses from the premises to the conclusion. The final *ought* then would read, "Other things being equal, Jones ought to pay Smith five dollars." The problem with this strategy is that, while it removes the troublesome evaluative principle from the premises, it changes the derivation from a categorical to a contingent proposition. Only *if* other things are equal ought Jones to pay Smith five dollars. Not only does the transformation run counter to Searle's intentions, but it makes the deduction the kind of arrangement Weber could have tolerated. Only by accepting without demonstrative proof some prior evaluative principle, that on which the *if* clause rests, can the *ought* be supported. It is important to understand, however, that the contingency is not necessarily an expression of wants. Weber relies heavily on *oughts* which are means to a desired end. Searle's transformed derivation rests instead on the acceptance of criteria which define extenuating circumstances. Whether Jones wants these particular criteria may be irrelevant without affecting the derivation. But the fact of contingency nevertheless weakens the derivation as a case against Hume's thesis, since it can be claimed that the contingency clause contains the unproved evaluative principle in the absence of which the derivation fails.[7]

The second strategy open to Searle leaves the *ceteris paribus* clauses in the premises, but regards the evaluative principle behind them as merely a state of affairs which can be described without endorsement. For example, Searle may maintain that whatever society accepts as *ceteris paribus* criteria can be incorporated into the derivation as descriptive statements in 3a and 4a. If, say, convention provides a defeat for promises when lives will be lost as a result of keeping a promise, then the *ceteris paribus* clause will state, among other things, that lives will not be lost if Jones pays Smith the five dollars. Such a criterion, in this second strategy open to Searle, will be described without an endorsement, binding only on the participants in the promising game. This is nothing more or less than how the institution of promising is accepted into the derivation. (One needn't approve of promising for the derivation to be valid.) This strategy is immune from positivist criticism, since if a positivist

---

[6]For a related point, see J. E. McClellan and B. P. Komisar, "On Deriving 'Ought' from 'Is,'" *Analysis*, 25 (1964), pp. 32–36.

[7]For a slightly different discussion of this point, see W. D. Hudson, *Modern Moral Philosophy* (New York: Doubleday & Company, Inc., 1970), pp. 287–91.

maintains that one must evaluate in describing either institutional facts or evaluative principles, then all possibility of doing neutral social science is denied; for neutrality rests precisely on the possibility of separating endorsements from descriptions on items such as these.

There are obvious differences between the constitutive rule of obligation which defines promising and the evaluative principle which establishes what counts in the *ceteris paribus* clauses, not least among these differences the fact that the rule of obligation in promising is not selected by those promising while the evaluative principle in *ceteris paribus* can be decided upon by those who promise. (I cannot choose not to be obligated and still promise, while I can logically choose anything as a criterion for defeating an obligation and still not go counter to the meaning of "obligation.") But it is still possible to describe both the *ceteris paribus* criteria and the act of promising without coming out in support of them. In such a case, the evaluative principle in *ceteris paribus* and the obligation in promising will extend on the participants only, on society or the individual. The effectiveness of this strategy, and even of the derivation, will then rest on how neatly one can separate observer and participant, and even whether binding propositions can be directed toward a participant on the basis of conventional rules.

2.1. The second objection to Searle's derivation arises from the center of the naturalistic controversy. It can be stated in the form of a rhetorical question. Is anyone bound to do anything by virtue of institutional arrangements or conceptual meanings? For the nonnaturalist, or positivist, the question is rhetorical because of the obvious *no* which answers it. Let us see again what Searle is proposing. From the fact of promising he derives an ought which prescribes keeping the promise. The ought follows necessarily from the institutional fact of promising, in that a denial of the *ought* will require a denial also of the description, i.e., no promise occurred if no ought follows. Conversely, if the description is accurate then the *ought* must follow. Let us allow that the ought binds only the participant in action, setting aside for the moment the issue of an observer-participant dichotomy. What is the source of bindingness for the one who promises? Obviously it is the institution of promising. The question the positivist would then ask is: Is one required to subscribe to the institution of promising? The answer the positivist gives is that no such requirement exists. To be bound by the institution of promising is to choose or decide to be bound. *This* choice or decision is the primary endorsement which provides for the deduction, and since it is freely entered into it can be denied without a logical contradiction. On this objection, the unsupported (or primary) *ought* which Hume's thesis requires is the affirmation of the institution of promising.

Suppose, to illustrate this point as strongly as possible, the Jones fellow in Searle's derivation is a member of an oppressive society which has managed to use the institution of promising to persecute innocent people. Let us further imagine that Jones is called before the ruling agency and asked to promise that he will reveal the names of all resisters to the state. Jones, a prudent man, readily promises, though secretly he vows to keep his own counsel on this issue. Now the naturalist, on the moral criteria by which we judge the society as oppressive and warrant Jones' secret vow, may decide either (a) that Jones did not promise even though he uttered the words "I promise" (Conditions C in Searle's derivation are not met), or (b) Jones promised but the promise is vitiated by the absence of a satisfactory fulfillment of *ceteris paribus* criteria. But if the naturalist chooses (a) then he is subject to a difficult question: If Jones has uttered all of the words which constitute the physicalist fact of promising, on what grounds can it be denied that he has made a promise? The answer which the positivist would provide for this question is that Jones has not accepted or endorsed the institution of promising in this instance. Put another way, the positivist would claim that it is possible logically to move from the physicalist fact of someone uttering a phonetic sequence to the institution of promising (from statement 1 to statement 2 in Searle's derivation) only with a suppressed premise on endorsement. It is this suppressed premise which provides for the nontautological proposition that one ought to keep one's promises, a vital ingredient in Searle's derivation; for without the endorsement one is not a subscribing member of the institution of promising and there is thus no force to the proposition that one ought to keep one's promises. If, however, the naturalist chooses (b), then he is placed in the awkward position of saying that a man promises even when coerced into doing so, that the voluntary character we ordinarily attach to promising is not really true, and that, in Searle's derivation, Conditions C do not cover the most fundamental quality of a promise—that those who are players in the promising game are in it on the basis of choosing and intending to promise.[8]

3. THE ISSUES RECONSIDERED

Though it is clear how Searle's derivation, and the objections to it, are important elements in any thorough discussion of values in social inquiry, it is not always easy to keep the issues separate. The following summary may be helpful.

---

[8]For the most persuasive statement of the nonnaturalist argument against Searle, see R. M. Hare, "The Promising Game," in W. D. Hudson, ed., *The Is-Ought Question*, pp. 144–56.

(a) Whether Searle's derivation succeeds or not, it is undeniable that the distinction between physicalist (or "brute") and institutional facts is important and, on the whole, missing in positivist social science. From physicalist descriptions no evaluative conclusion can be drawn. Institutional facts do provide the grounds for deriving values, though whether this derivation proceeds from purely nonevaluative premises is, as we have seen, an issue of some dispute. One consequence which seems to follow from this distinction in kinds of facts is that the phenomena of the natural world are not wholly continuous with social phenomena, in that the latter contain institutional facts while the former contain only physicalist facts. Whether this means a parallel discontinuity in the application of natural science techniques to the study of society cannot be answered here, but it is undeniable that additional factors must be considered when social events are the objects of study.

(b) Again regardless of the validity of Searle's derivation, the simple distinction assumed in positivist social science between description and evaluation must be amended. The statement "Jones promised to pay Smith five dollars" is a description on all criteria of description accepted by social scientists. It does not contain first-order evaluative terms like *right, good, ought,* or second-order terms like *courage.* It is not a commendation, an expression of favor, an endorsement. How the speaker feels about promising is irrelevant to the statement. Nor is it a statement which intends an effect on the listener of favor or disfavor. Were the statement framed independent of the derivation at issue any social scientist would pronounce it a fit and healthy description, a fact if verified as true. Yet it yields, steadily or unsteadily, a deduced *ought.* If the positivist view is to be effectively maintained, some new criteria for identifying and demarcating facts and values is needed.

(c) However Hume's thesis (so basic to modern social science) can be shored up and rearranged, the fact remains that the thesis as orginally stated and generally understood by social scientists today has been struck a blow. No recovery, no matter how remarkable, can deny that. As usually accepted, the thesis denies that an *ought* can be derived from *any* set of purely descriptive statements. The statement on promising is, as we have seen, a description on the criteria of description generally accepted by those who endorse Hume's thesis. To say that it is a special kind of description, an institutional fact, or that it is a description only from the point of view of an observer, thus qualifying it for Hume's thesis, is a qualification nowhere to be found in the writings of Hume or his supporters prior to Searle's contribution. So at the very least the thesis of a logical separation between *is* and *ought* must be seen as having a different meaning with different kinds of facts.

(d) The validity of Searle's derivation seems to depend on the positions taken on two issues. These are (1) the effectiveness with which the observer can be distinguished from the participant in social action, and (2) the degree to which we are free to accept or reject the social arrangements through which we have human experiences. If it is possible to maintain a detachment which yet permits language to remain social and not physicalist, then institutional facts may be descriptive without committing the one describing to an endorsement. If such detachment is impossible, then description and evaluation are inexorably mixed in the utterance of certain factual statements. This is the first issue. On the second issue, if institutions depend for their effect on a freely given endorsement, then *oughts* drawn from institutional rules are dependent on this volitional action and are deduced only from a prior choice (as Hume and his descendants maintain). On the other hand, if some institutions are necessary conditions for the possibility of human life, not chosen but required for experience to take place at all, then *oughts* do follow deductively from the description of such institutions. All of the criticisms of Searle seem to rest on a position taken on one of these two issues, and we will now explore them anew from a different direction.

4. EXPLANATION AND MORAL EVALUATION

Charles Taylor argues persuasively against the positivist version of political inquiry.[9] Taylor's case can be seen as consisting of three claims, all distinct though comprising a continuous argument. The first is a demonstration that explanation and evaluation affect one another in important ways. For Taylor, any explanatory theory tells us (in the form of its "conceptual structure") what needs to be explained, how (or by what factors) the explanation is to be made, and the dimensions through which the phenomena can vary. For example, the principle of inertia in the physical sciences will identify matter, state the terms on which the movement of matter is to be accounted for, and legislate a range of possible variations for bodies. Anything outside these specifications will not be taken seriously, e.g., Aristotle's teleological framework.

An explanation, for Taylor, will always constrain evaluations by virtue of the fact that it makes claims on experience. Aristotle's explanatory framework, for example, claims permanence for class conflict. This explanation is incompatible with Plato's normative theory of the state, which includes an end to class conflict. Accepting Aristotle's explanatory theory makes it impossible to accept Plato's normative theory as a feasible possiblity, as accepting the feasibility of Plato's normative theory requires rejecting the truth of Aristotle's explanatory theory. Or, put another way,

[9]Charles Taylor, "Neutrality in Political Science," in P. Laslett and W. Runciman, eds., *Politics, Philosophy and Society,* third series (Oxford: Basil Blackwell, 1967).

Aristotle's explanation, if true, makes Plato's theory *utopian;* Plato's theory, if feasible, makes Aristotle's theory *false.* In opposition to the naive positivist thought that facts (explanations) and values (normative theory) are independent of one another, Taylor suggests that the two logically constrain one another.

The second claim Taylor makes is that the logic of the predicate *good* prohibits it from being used as the primary premise of an evaluative claim, as is necessary in Hume's thesis. It is commonly thought that the term *good* is used to commend. This thought, as we have seen, is vital to a neutral social science, where it is held that an elimination of such first-order terms from social science will also effectively remove commendations (evaluations). For Taylor, the use of *good* may or may not be to commend, but the commendatory function of *good* is not as important to the issue of scientific neutrality as the fact that to use *good* is always to claim that there are reasons for commending whatever the term is applied to.

One may recognize a variety of emotive expressions for communicating a positive state of mind. An appreciative nod, a grunt of approval, a statement of likes, all of these and more may function to convey an affirmative stance. None require rational support. To say, for example, "I like *X,*" may be the first and last word on the subject, short of a psychosociological history of the emotion. One is not required normally to justify one's likes. To say that *X* is good, on the other hand, is to say something that does seem to require justification. It is not the end of things, as an expression of likes may be, but an assertion which must be supported by reasons. Only, in fact, as judgments of goodness *are* supported by reasons can they be distinguished from purely emotive expressions of the sort described above. Thus *good* cannot be the first emotive expression in evaluative discourse, the nonrational evaluation on which all further *oughts* depend (as required in Hume's thesis), for we must always be able to advance rational support for *good* judgments. They are never nonrational first premises, but rather supervenient on other propositions which function as reasons.

The immediate implication of this view of the logic of *good* judgments is that another connection between evaluation and explanation has been provided. On the first of Taylor's claims explanation was seen to constrain the feasibility range of evaluations. On this, the second of his claims, evaluations require rational support in order to be evaluations and not mere expressions of emotion. It is obvious that reasons for action must be propositions which are well-supported empirically, since to offer false or dubious propositions as reasons is not really to provide a justification. It is equally obvious that an explanatory theory, which consists of general propositions which have withstood at least some measure of empirical testing, is an excellent source for supporting reasons. Thus evaluations are constrained by explanations, but also properly rest on explanations for their justification; for an evaluation supported by a comprehensive and sound explanatory theory must, by virtue of what we mean by an explanatory theory, have the securest foundation of reasons possible.

Taylor also advances a third claim in his argument, one which asserts for some factual statements a *prima facie* connection, as reasons, to judgments of goodness. For Taylor, to say of something that it fulfills human wants, needs, or purposes always constitutes a reason for calling that something good. Taylor does not commit the fallacy attributed to naturalists who say that good *means* some state of affairs, which in Taylor's case would be "conducive to human needs, wants, purposes." Thus he escapes the logical point scored by nonnaturalists who point out that the denial that any defining state of affairs is good will not lead to a contradiction, as we may say logically that what is conducive to human wants, needs, purposes is *not* good without uttering a contradiction (as we would utter if we say "All bachelors are *not* unmarried men"). What Taylor is interested in is how the denial of what is conducive to human wants, needs, purposes, can be effected given the purely logical point that it can be without a contradiction.

Taylor allows that these are two kinds of objection to an evaluation. One he calls *overriding,* where the evaluation is accepted but curtailed by more important considerations. Free speech, for example, is a value we might readily accept, yet limit in certain circumstances because of the overriding consideration of, say, public safety. Justice Oliver Wendell Holmes' famous restriction on the freedom of anyone to scream fire in a crowded theatre is an example of an overriding evaluation. An overriding evaluation is not directed at the value being overridden. Free speech is not denigrated, or invalidated, or even criticized with Holmes' declaration. It is merely subordinated to a higher value, public safety, on certain occasions. An *undermining* evaluation, on the other hand, is one where the status of an evaluation is denied, perhaps even the very properties by which a thing is judged good are dismissed. To say, for example, that free speech prevents authentic social harmony where social harmony is deemed necessary to any version of the good life is, in effect, to deny that free speech is worthwhile.

Now there are two points crucial to Taylor's third claim here. The first is that anything which is conducive to human wants, needs, purposes is *prima facie* good. It stands as justified unless an effort is made to show that it is not. The second point is that each of the two kinds of objection to an evaluation will have different effects on the explanatory framework supporting the evaluation. An overriding objection will set aside the evaluation but not touch the supporting explanation, while an undermining objection is a challenge also to the explanation. Curtailing free speech in crowded theatres, for example, requires no assertion on that which justifies free speech. Denying the worthiness of free speech, on the other hand, will be successful only if the explanatory propositions supporting free speech are discredited.

Let's take the first point. To support it Taylor is committed to saying that some descriptive statements function as their own justifications. This is not a hard proposition to swallow. We can marshall many commonplace assertions to support it. To describe something as a legal action, for example, seems already to invest it with warrantability. The example used by Taylor is instructive. When we describe the activity commonly called "doctoring" as aimed at healing, we are uttering a descriptive statement which carries with it its own justification: It *can* be denied, but not without some countervailing arguments. To say, "Doctors aim at killing" is to say something which demands justification. It cannot stand without support as the contrary proposition linking doctoring and healing can so stand. Unless supported, the proposition on doctoring to kill risks the status of lunacy. Again, such observations do not deny that a case can be made for the doctoring-to-kill proposition. It is merely to point out that the justification is required to establish the sensibility of the assertion, while the doctoring-to-heal proposition is justified in itself.

Taylor relies on this kind of connection, grounded on ordinary standards of sensibility, in claiming for the proposition "conducive to human wants, needs, purposes" a *prima facie* status of goodness. Again, Taylor does not say that *good* means this (or any) proposition. He claims rather that the use of the term *good* is unintelligible outside of any reference to the proposition, in that the reasons on which a judgment of goodness is supervenient imply statements to the effect that the X judged as good is conducive to human wants, needs, purposes. Similarly, to say that something is conducive to human wants, needs, purposes is to say something already justified as good unless countervailing considerations are offered and triumph over the *prima facie* force of the initial proposition. Countervailing considerations, as we have seen, are either overriding or undermining. An overriding objection would set aside the proposition on human wants, needs, purposes for certain circumstances while not challenging its worthiness. An undermining objection would challenge the proposition itself with a denial of the value of fulfilling human wants, needs, purposes. For example, to say that children ought to be fed an adequate diet is surely an instance of this kind of *prima facie* good. But it can be overridden, as might be rationally decided in conditions where resources are so scarce that to feed children adequately means that all adults will starve to death. It is more difficult to imagine an undermining objection, it seeming to challenge the very *prima facie* status of wants, needs, and purposes which makes possible the two kinds of objection. But even this is possible, say where the proposition is objected to on the grounds that serving God is the principle for *good* judgments, not fulfilling human wants, needs, or purposes. The thing to notice about an undermining objection on such an occasion is that it requires an alteration in the ordinary standards of sensibility which do give *prima facie* goodness to the proposition on human wants, needs, purposes.

It follows that propositions on human wants, needs, purposes are the mediating devices between explanation and evaluation. If *good* judgments are supervenient on reasons, and reasons for such judgments imply statements on wants, needs, purposes, then one can infer an evaluation from an explanatory theory only by reference to a proposition on wants, needs, purposes. Further, Taylor asserts that every explanatory framework requires a schedule of human wants, needs, purposes, in that every general statement of fact on social phenomena will rest on assumptions about what men want or need or have as purposes. Thus these key factors serve as the conveyor belts between fact and value, and themselves function as *prima facie* principles for evaluations.

5. MORAL CHOICE AND MORAL NECESSITY

It is helpful, in assessing Taylor's argument, to see where it stands against the positivist version of social science. Like Searle, one of Taylor's important contributions is a revised view of facts. Searle, it will be recalled, relied on a distinction between institutional and physicalist (or "brute") facts. Taylor relies on a *prima facie* ranking of facts. Those states of affairs conducive to the fulfillment of human wants, needs, or purposes are *prima facie* good. They rank higher on a scale of worthiness than do states of affairs which are irrelevant to the fulfillment of wants, needs, purposes, and certainly higher than those states of affairs which deny such a fulfillment. Again, rational argument may invert the given order of facts. But, for Taylor, there *is* a given order which, in the ordinary world of human experience, provides for evaluations prior to judgment. For the positivist, all facts are equal in being without evaluative qualities. Or, turned around, a positivist sees no values in facts until the perceiving subject assigns value through judgment. Taylor's facts come to the perceiving subject rich with value, scaled for worthiness, and stand in a natural hierarchy unless effort is made to rearrange them.

Taylor has also reminded us that *good* has a grammar of its own not reducible to the logic of purely emotive expressions. Weber defined all evaluations as endorsements, which largely meant expressions of favor.

It is notorious that positivism has been unable to furnish a successful formulation of evaluative expressions. On the one hand, the positivist thesis on values, that they are not statable as verifiable propositions (see Chapter One), requires that values be some sort of emotive expression. On the other hand, the range of emotive expressions for evaluation is vast and complex, and none seem adequately to sum up the function of *good* judgments. Certainly the primitive term *like* does not do justice to *good*. I can easily say that *X* is good but I do not like *X*. ("Exercise is good, but I do not like to do it.") If this is so, then we cannot reduce goodness to likes without losing whatever it is in *good* judgments which is not covered in *like* expressions. Weber's endorsements, or expressions of favor, fare no better as synonyms for *good*. If they are to be distinguished from *likes* it must be on the basis of some more informed state of mind, say an expression of approval. But even this is subject to the same critique. Something may be good *for* someone without his knowing it and thus having a chance to approve of it, as when we talk of good in terms of interest. (The presence of atmospheric shielding is good for human beings, but its goodness—in protecting life from excessive radiation from outer space—does not depend upon approval of any sort.) Taylor, with others, sees *good* as distinguished from emotive expressions in being supervenient on reasons, thus separating it out from the positivist grab bag of noncognitivist terms.

5.1. Is Taylor's case against positivist social science effective? It is important to notice that part of Taylor's argument, that demonstrating the constraint that explanation has on the feasibility of evaluations, can be incorporated into a revised social science without dropping the substance of Weber's views. Only a very naive supporter of Weber would maintain that facts and values are in all ways independent of one another, for even Weber allowed as how scientific analysis can elucidate and inform value judgments. But, on the other hand, the revisions required by Taylor's arguments should not go unnoticed. He has demonstrated that just any choice of an *ought* will not do, that some values can be ruled out by virtue of what we know about the world. So Weber's strict view that knowledge itself is never sufficient to tell us what we ought to do must be restated in Taylor's thesis to mean that knowledge nevertheless can reveal some *oughts* as feasible and others not, thus telling us what we ought not to bother to try. So, at the very least, the view that all primary *oughts* are nonrational must be revised, for some are more rational as possible courses of action than others.

This differential rationality of evaluations is reinforced with the view of *good* as supervenient on reasons. Though not original with Taylor (something to which he readily accedes), this point of view on evaluations will always provide that evaluations can be ranked according to the kind and scope of evidence which can be marshalled to support them. This is a view difficult to deny. The ordinary uses of *good* seem markedly rational in this respect, something expressions of *like* are not. But it is not certain that the ordinary supervenience of *good* on reasons will logically rule out its functioning as a primary nonrational evaluation. One thing which has to be recognized is that the word *good* has a variety of uses. One way of categorizing these uses is by separating those which depend on accepted evaluative criteria and those which establish evaluative criteria. In the first use, when we say that something is good, we are grading it on the basis of the evaluative criteria for such items. "This is good car" is a judgment that a certain car, this car, fulfills the standards which make cars good. It is not a judgment on the standards themselves. In the second use of good, we affirm the standards themselves as good, setting them up to use in grading items of a certain sort. To say, for example, that a braking system which stops the car quickly, high gas mileage, fast acceleration, and so on, count as what makes a car good, is to use good in the criteria-setting sense.

Now the difference between Taylor and the kind of social science assumptions we have identified with Weber must occur on the criteria-setting use of *good*. The use of *good* when criteria are already settled is too straightforward to divide naturalists and nonnaturalists, since it is characterized by pigeon-holing judgments consistent with either of the two philosophical positions. The devisive question is, where do the criteria come from? Weber and those who comprise his legacy assert that we choose or affirm the criteria. On such a view, the supervenience of *good* on reasons can itself be sustained only by allowing for a primary nonrational use of good, that use which establishes the system of rules and evidence which permits propositions to count as reasons. Taylor seems to feel, on the other hand, that the criteria are given in experience, not established through choice or affirmation. For Weber and other nonnaturalists, effort is needed to bring about evaluative criteria. For Taylor, effort is required to change them from what they naturally are. Given this difference between Taylor and the positivist legacy, it is clear that Taylor cannot deny that *good* functions as a primary noncognitive premise simply by asserting the supervenience of *good* on reasons, for the criteria which make propositions reasons must themselves by justified. He denies such a use for *good* with the larger (and more important) claim that the primary evaluative *good* is presented by experience itself.

This brings the assessment of Taylor home to his reliance on the *prima facie* good of anything conducive to human wants, needs, or purposes. Can *this* function as the primary evaluative criterion? One thing which seems wrong immediately with Taylor's formula is the possibility that each of the words in the key phrase, "wants, needs, purposes," may be contrary to any of the others. This is especially important with the first two words, wants and needs. It is reasonable to assume that a need may override a want, though there is no indication on the order of priority if and when they do conflict. Given the possibility of internal conflict, however, a reliance on the blanket phrase "wants, needs, or purposes" may itself be an inconsistency in evaluation.

Even more important, however, Taylor offers us no specification of what these three terms mean. The nonnaturalist will point out, against Taylor, that two people will be able to agree on the assertion that anything conducive to human wants, needs, purposes is good, but then disagree on what is to count as a human want, need, or purpose. In short, the terms advanced as evaluative criteria are sufficiently vague so that contrary evaluations may be consistent with them. In terms of the naturalistic controversy, we have not been offered any facts, *prima facie* or decisive, which function as premises for deriving evaluations. Even worse, we do not have the standards required for criteria-dependent *good* judgments, and thus, in effect, no evaluative criteria. The crippling nature of this point can be seen quite clearly when we reflect on how evaluative criteria operate normally. As in the earlier example on cars, they provide the basis for settling on a correct or valid evaluation. If we transfer Taylor's type of criteria to cars, it would be possible to judge any particular car as good *or* bad on the *same* criteria of evaluation.

Taylor's case for self-justifying criteria assumes for experience, and language, a reality which the subject discovers. Like the example of doctoring, this reality is altered evaluatively only with rational effort. But even the *prima facie* status of this reality in an evaluative matrix is questionable. An undermining objection will, according to Taylor, rearrange the explanatory framework of an evaluation, which is tantamount to saying that it will rearrange its conception of reality. If an undermining objection can be successfully directed at a proposition conducive to the fulfillment of human wants, needs, purposes, then the reality (or conception of experience) underlying that evaluation is altered. To state the now familiar analogy: The denial that healing is worthwhile challenges the very activity of doctoring. If such challenges are possible, however, and capable of success, then we have no reality to discover. It is a reality made up of concepts and points of view, shifting with the perspective brought to bear on experience, and this subject-dependent reality is precisely what the positivists have been arguing all along.

These remarks do not discredit Taylor's argument so much as they illuminate its foundation. This foundation should be familiar to us by now, even though it has remained fugitive to any conclusive assessment. It can be stated in the form of questions parallel to the issues raised in the discussion of Searle's derivation. Are there principles we may discover which provide premises to evaluative discourse? Or are fundamental oughts chosen? Is a free detachment from social reality possible? Or is there a given quality to experience (and language) which makes us all agents (not observers) and which compels certain evaluative conclusions?

Though no satisfactory answer may ever be given to these questions, it takes little acumen to see that discussing them further carries us into three important areas. The first consists of those traditions found in most societies which do provide criteria for evaluations, criteria which are not chosen for the moment by the participant *or* observer. Law, as we shall see, provides such criteria. The second area is moral evaluation, where it is often claimed that there are at least higher values, if not incorrigible ones, to be discovered. The third area is the set of arrangements through which society *does* impose values, thus creating a necessity not always happily established in evaluative reasoning.

FOR FURTHER READING

Foot, Philippa, ed. *Theories of Ethics.* Oxford: Oxford University Press, 1967.

Hare, R. M. *The Language of Morals.* Oxford: Oxford University Press, 1952.

_____. *Freedom and Reason.* New York: Oxford University Press, 1965.

Hudson, W. D. *Modern Moral Philosophy.* New York: Doubleday & Company, Inc., 1970.

_____, ed. *The Is-Ought Question.* New York: St. Martin's Press, Inc., 1969.

Hume, David. *An Inquiry Concerning the Principles of Morals.* New York: The Liberal Arts Press, 1957.

Kerner, George. *The Revolution in Ethical Theory.* Oxford: Oxford University Press, 1966.

Nowell-Smith, P. H. *Ethics.* Baltimore: Penguin Books, Inc., 1954.

Searle, J. R. *Speech Acts.* Cambridge: Cambridge University Press, 1969.

_____, ed. *The Philosophy of Language.* Oxford: Oxford University Press, 1971.

Stevenson, Charles. *Ethics and Language.* New Haven: Yale University Press, 1944.

CHAPTER THREE

EVALUATION IN LAW

1. RULES IN SOCIAL EVENTS

One way to relate the issues identified in the first two chapters to the more concrete concerns of social or political inquiry is to see social events as institutional facts, with all of the features marking such facts off from physicalist facts. It is unlikely that many ordinary social events will have rules as precise as those defining formal activities like chess, where all of the rules (though not all of the strategies) can be stated in rulebooks, nor rules as singular as the rule of obligation constituting the promising game. Yet many kinds of social phenomena are understandable *as* social, as district from physical phenomena, only as we see them in terms of some set of rules or another.

It may seem that this assertion is nothing more than a play on the word "rules," since it is well-known that physical events are explained quite easily with systems of rules. What could be a clearer case of "ruled" activity than the movement of the planets in our solar system, summed up so neatly in Kepler's laws of planetary motion? If we examine the laws explaining the movement of the planets, however, we will quickly discover that they are rules only for those who are trying to account for the planets' movement. There is no sense in which Kepler's laws "govern" or prescribe for the planets, and no sense in which the planets follow the laws. Obviously if we discover that the planets are not accounted for by our explanatory laws we do not judge the planets "wrong" (as we might well do with moral laws). We merely reformulate the laws to account for this change.

It is true that this subordination of explanatory laws to the phenomena being explained is found also in social science. Laws purporting to explain the behavior of an electorate, for example, are altered, even dismissed as false or inadequate, if they fail to account for the way voters behave. But there is also a second system of rules in social inquiry which is not found in the physical sciences. Unlike planets, people *are* governed by, and follow, rules. So that which is studied by social scientists, unlike that which is studied by physical scientists, has its own body of rules. These rules, furthermore, can be prescriptive on the events as explanatory laws cannot be. Thus, while the rules comprising explanation in the physical and social sciences may be identical (as in rules of inference and evidence), and while these rules may bind the scientist similarly in both types of inquiry, social events still present a second order of rules *in* the phenomena which physical events do not.[1]

We have seen how rules in human action can be distinguished according to whether they constitute an activity in the sense that the activity cannot occur without the rules (as in chess rules), or whether they regulate a preexisting activity (as etiquette rules regulate eating). We may add to this account the distinction outlined in the paragraph above, that rules can be either prescriptive or descriptive. The rules of most games, for example, state what one must do to play the game, and allow for judgments that someone is breaking the rules. Purely descriptive rules do not state what one must or ought to do, and thus there is no sense in which descriptive rules are "broken." On the other hand, we often do use the term "rules" in a descriptive sense, as in "As a rule, people would rather buy cheap and sell dear." In this latter use of rules, an orderly or systematic pattern of behavior is stated as a rule which people follow or which can be used as a device to account for their behavior.

Though both types of rule classification, constitutive-regulative and prescriptive-descriptive, are helpful in understanding social action, two mistakes must be avoided in seeing society as systems of rules. The first mistake is thinking that all social action is rule-following. Breaking a rule is obviously not following a rule, and though we may want to account for the deviant player in terms of a rule, the fact remains that such a player need not be following any rule. Random or aimless behavior is also not rule-following. Taking a stroll in the park, letting whims govern, just doing what the moment suggests—language contains a variety of expressions for rule-less actions. Some theories of action want to claim rules even for actions such as these, as certain interpreters of Freud would argue that even aimlessness has its unconscious direction, and strolling in the park may be governed by laws no less fundamental just because they are hidden to the agent. But the point of allowing rule-less actions

[1]For an expansion of this observation, see Peter Winch, *The Idea of a Social Science* (New York: Humanities Press, 1958).

into our understanding of society is that playing chess and strolling in the park seem substantially different precisely on whether the agent in each case is following rules. To say that all action is rule-following will not reflect, and thus account for, this obvious difference. Further, though what it means for someone to follow a rule is a complicated matter, some kinds of social action do not seem to be covered even by rules unknown to the agent. It has been pointed out, for example, that inventions cannot be predicted because if they could be they would not be inventions. Creative actions, or those impossible to anticipate, seem rule-less by definition.[2]

The second mistake is a converse version of the first. Even where the notion of a rule *is* appropriate, we must not think that the rules which account for social action are always known or the results of intended action by the members of a society. The stock market, for example, is an institution defined by certain rules. Yet the full meaning of this institution, a complete inventory of its rules, will not be found by surveying the members of the institution, or even necessarily the members of the society in which the institution is located. A theory of economics is required. In other cases some psychological theory may be needed to complete the account of an agent's action, something which even the agent may acknowledge when confronted (as in psychoanalysis) with a statement on the origins of his actions. Even in trying to understand a formal game, where the rules are explicit and accessible, the players may be far less helpful than a rule book. So to say that social action is distinctive in being rule-following does not mean (1) that *all* social action is rule-governed, or (2) that even when rules define social action that such rules must be known or understood by those who engage in the action.

2. LAW AS AN INSTITUTIONAL FACT

Legal behavior, or action which is describable in terms of legal concepts, is obviously rule-following or rule-governed action. We may act in accordance with the law either consciously (following the rule of law) or habitually (being governed by the rule of law without necessarily reflecting on it). But in either case behavior is understandable only in terms of the rules. Whether law is comprised mainly of constitutive or regulative rules is less certain, since some actions seem to have no meaning apart from the legal language which describes them (as in filing a will) while other actions seem to preexist and then be regulated by law (as "killing" ante-

[2]Karl Popper, "Indeterminism in Quantum Physics," *The British Journal for the Philosophy of Science,* Vol. 1, Nos. 2 and 3 (1950).

dates and is regulated by the term "murder"). Still another distinction in kinds of rules is helpful. Practice rules may be marked off from summary rules, where in the latter case rules are drawn from activities.[3] Chess, baseball, logic are all defined by practice rules. The rules of medicine and engineering, on the other hand, are descriptive summaries of a class of actions past and present. Practice rules would seem always to be constitutive. Summary rules, on the other hand, may be either constitutive (as in strategy rules for chess, which cannot exist except in terms of chess) or regulative (as the rules of engineering regulate a preexisting activity). Law seems describable in terms of summary rules, for unlike formal games like chess the law is fundamentally conditioned and formed by what people decide and how they act over time.

It *is* certain, however, that legal language is a hybrid of description and prescription. Any legal system will reflect to some degree the behavior of its members, for it is unimaginable that conventional law can be at total variance with conventional behavior. (Unlike moral laws, the fact that people are not obeying the laws of a society counts as a reason for changing the law, as with Prohibition. Where the reason does not prevail, as in murders or gambling, a moral issue is typically involved.) But the law also prescribes conduct. It tells us what we ought to do, or establishes the ground rules for what we do. It is this combination of description and prescription which allows law to function as a device both to anticipate behavior and to regulate it.

2.1. If we view law as an institutional fact, as an arrangement of action in terms of rules in the way discussed above, then the issues discussed earlier take on a new dimension. It should be noticed that legal language is typically a second-order evaluation. As pointed out above, it both describes and evaluates. To describe someone as a murderer, for example, is also to condemn him. As with other second-order evaluations, the descriptive and evaluative components are ordinarily separable. The act of murder can be stated as a physicalist description, that someone did certain things which can be described independent of any institution (in terms of bodily movements, for example), which then counts within a legal system as the institutional fact of murder. We saw that one important problem Searle encounters in deriving *ought* from *is* is moving, without a premise on endorsement, from the physicalist fact of someone uttering a phonetic sequence to the institutional fact of promising. The important issue here is whether the institutional facts of a legal system provide a more adequate connection between physicalist facts and institutional facts, so that the evaluative component of an insti-

---

[3]John Rawls, "Two Concepts of Rules," *Philosophical Review*, Vol. 64 (1955), pp. 3–32, though Rawls does not view summary rules as constitutive on occasion (as I do here).

tutional fact is more securely grounded in purely descriptive propositions.

Instead of the act of promising, let us consider the act of entering a legal contract. Jones, the key figure in the promising game, this time makes a purchase offer on Smith's house. He "promises" in the form of a legally binding proposal to buy Smith's house for $50,000. To see the differences between the promising game and the legal game, let's arrange the statements in the same general form of Searle's derivation.

1. Jones wrote the words "I hereby offer to buy Smith's house for $50,000" and affixed his signature under the words.
2. Jones made a purchase offer of $50,000 on Smith's house.
3. Jones placed himself under (undertook) an obligation to purchase Smith's house for $50,000.
4. Jones is under an obligation to purchase Smith's house for $50,-000.
5. Jones ought to purchase Smith's house for $50,000.

As with the promising game, additional statements are needed to complete the derivation. They are as follows:

Between 1 and 2:
  1a. Under certain conditions C anyone who writes the words (sentence) 'I hereby offer to buy Smith's house for $50,000' and affixes his signature to the statement makes a purchase offer on Smith's house for $50,000.
  1b. Conditions C obtain.
Between 2 and 3:
  2a. All purchase offers are acts of placing oneself under (undertaking) an obligation to purchase the item toward which the purchase offer is made at the price offered.
Between 3 and 4:
  3a. Other things are equal.
  3b. All those who place themselves under an obligation are, other things being equal, under an obligation.
Between 4 and 5:
  4a. Other things are equal.
  4b. Other things being equal, one ought to do what one is under an obligation to do.

As with the Searle derivation, a number of critical strategies can be directed at this sequence of statements. But the one of most interest here is that criticism which was especially telling against Searle: that the move from statement 1 to statement 2 can be made only with a suppressed premise on endorsement. The agent, Jones, must be sincere about his promise; he must, in the more general sense, choose to be a member of the promising game; and this is the primary evaluation which permits the derivation of an *ought*. Notice, however, how the derivation of the legal *ought* in the sequence of statements above is immune from this criticism. It is irrelevant whether Jones is sincere about his offer, or whether he is in any particular state of mind when he signs the purchase offer. Or, put another way, the public criteria of the written statement suffices as sufficient proof for the state of mind. No additional mentalistic proposition is needed. This point can be stated even more strongly. Unlike the utterance of the phonetic sequence in the promising game, the physicalist fact of writing the linguistic sequence and affixing a signature in the way described above *is* equivalent to the institutional fact of a contract. The move from statement 1 to statement 2 can be made without the suppressed premise on endorsement, for endorsement is satisfied with the physicalist description. A legal *ought,* in short, can be derived from an *is* without an additional premise on the agent's sincerity in performing the act.

It is possible to succeed with the derivation of a legal obligation (and *ought*) where the promising game falters because of the public character of performances defining many legal acts. Searle's derivation depends upon a semantic theory of language which provides for what have been called "illocutionary" utterances.[4] An illocutionary utterance is an utterance in which the speaker does something in saying the statement beyond merely saying the statement. He does what the statement says. To say, for example, "I warn you" or "I command you" is to do what the statement specifies as the statement is uttered, i.e., to warn or command. It is commonly accepted that promising is an illocutionary expression. To say, "I promise," seems not only to utter a statement, but to do something in uttering the statement, i.e., to promise. Illocutionary statements are obviously different from locutionary statements, as "That table is red," where the statement may be uttered without the speaker doing anything but uttering the statement. That promising is an illocutionary expression is impossible to deny. But, unlike some other kinds of illocutionary expressions, promising seems to require an additional performance on the part of the agent, where the agent does promise in uttering the words "I promise" only on condition of his sincerity. "I command you" does not, for example, seem so reliant on the agent's state of mind.

[4]The phrase originates with John Austin. See *How to Do Things with Words* (London: Oxford, Clarendon Press, 1962), pp. 94–107.

The important feature of legal language, seen as an institutional fact, is that it provides a range of "strong" illocutionary statements, where the performance of the act is coextensive with the uttering of the statement, and no additional condition on the state of mind of the agent is required for the performance. To say, for example, "I thee wed" in the proper setting is to wed, is to become married. Setting aside coercion with a *ceteris paribus* clause, one can imagine the comic possibilities if one of the participants in a marriage ceremony claimed the marriage wasn't authentic, didn't count, because he really didn't mean the words when he said them. One simply *is* married by virtue of the public criteria of written and spoken word. In promising, a provision always seems reserved for state of mind qualifications, which may prevent the phonetic sequence "I promise" from actually being a promise. Marriage is legally contracted on the phonetic and written sequences alone, which in the proper setting will be all that is required to make a marriage binding.

Of course it is undeniable that the promising game, the contract game, certainly the marriage game the way it is currently played, are alike in requiring the absence of coercion for validity. If Jones is forced to speak or sign his name, he is normally under no moral or legal obligation on the issue which is forced. Some laws, resting on "strict liability," exclude all excepting conditions, but some element of freedom of action is a common feature of legal obligations. Notice, however, how promising and an ordinary legal contract continue to differ even when this similarity is accepted. For one thing, there is a sense in which excepting conditions are accepted by the party who promises, while excepting conditions for legal contracts are normally not something that the individual accepts or declines. They are matters of public record, often written into the institution of law, and have binding force whether any given party to a contract affirms them or not. For another thing, and to some extent a consequence of the first difference, what it is which makes something a contract is an institutional matter, not depending on an individual endorsement for validity. What makes a certain phonetic sequence a promise, however, seems in some way dependent on the individual intending it as a promise, endorsing the act as an instance of promise-keeping. A man who doesn't intend to promise, as a state of mind, doesn't ordinarily promise. A man who marries is taken as intending to marry by virtue of uttering the right words. No state of mind is required beyond the public utterance.

Now it may be said against these remarks that mental concepts do not in fact refer to anything at all, and are thus nonsense language.[5] For someone to have an intention to promise he has to understand and be a member of the promising game in the first place. Jones can demur from

[5]This is the view Wittgenstein developed in *Philosophical Investigations*.

promising only as a game member, and in any case the proof of his nonendorsement must be public criteria and not some "private" mental state. Against this objection it can be pointed out that someone may be in the promising game but not of it, playing his own game to his own advantage. A systematic actor may act out, perform in the theatrical sense the action of promising, yet never promise in the sense that he takes on the obligation which the words seem to create. The proof of his nonmembership may be criteria as public as that demonstrating obligation, consisting of written demurrals, spoken asides, any of a number of things which demonstrate the absence of endorsement. Such a man is not playing the promising game even though he goes through the illocutionary movements. The point where law can be different is that in contractual actions such demurrals and reservations ordinarily do not count. All the evidence of good faith a contract may require is in the contract itself, in the performance. One cannot pretend to be getting married when the setting is right (in a church, say, before a minister), going through the legal motions but holding back an endorsement. The endorsement is in the legal motions, not issued from the players; and so the obligation is incurred from the actions of the game, not from the conjunction of the game and an additional premise on the agent's state of mind. There are, on the other hand, no comparably right settings for a promise, nothing as formal as churches and ministers to set the stage for an obligation. The intentions of the promiser cannot be inferred from the setting, as the intentions of a contracting party can be. So the promising game, unlike the contractual game, seems to be a collection of several games, prominent among this collection the intentions of the agent (one game) and the institutional performances of promising (another game). The contractual game, on the other hand, seems more tailored to a single game, the contract, where the institutional performance is all and nothing relevant occurs offstage.

2.2. One important difference between naturalists and positivists is how each explains the establishment of evaluative criteria. Earlier (Chapter Two) a distinction was made between criteria-establishing evaluations and criteria-dependent evaluations. In evaluating any item we depend upon criteria of evaluation, as judging an automobile as good or bad requires that we have some criteria of goodness for automobiles. "This is a good car" is a criteria-dependent evaluation. There can be little difference between naturalists and positivists on the logic of criteria-dependent evaluations, since they are no more than judgments that some particular item fulfills, or fails to fulfill, whatever criteria are used to evaluate the item. But on the origin of evaluative criteria there can be, and are, substantial disagreements. A naturalist, as we saw in the discussion of Taylor, will argue that evaluative criteria are discovered or encountered in experience. Plato, for example, claimed that the principles of justice are discovered, not chosen. Like mathematical truths, Plato's principles are revealed to the inquiring agents. A positivist, on the other hand, will argue that evaluative criteria are chosen, established by the endorsement of the agent. So Weber argues, as we have seen, that any primary *ought* may be chosen (or affirmed), and rational action begins after the establishment of this *ought.*

This difference between naturalists and positivists on the origin of evaluative criteria also leads to different views on the truth-value of first principles. To positivists, as we have seen, primary value statements do not make truth claims, while to naturalists they do. Each of these theses follows from the position taken on the origin of evaluative criteria. Think for a moment of the difference between discovering the right answer to a mathematical equation and deciding which movie to see on an evening out. The first action is governed by the criteria of mathematics, which allows a validity judgment on any answer given. The second is governed by no validity criteria. A decision can be warranted or unwarranted, but not true-false or right-wrong. To say, therefore, that evaluative criteria are *discovered* is to invest in truth-criteria which legislate claims. Saying that evaluative criteria are outcomes of *decisions* is effectively to exclude truth-criteria.

In assessing the relative merits of two contrary arguments it is often illuminating to see them in terms of concrete cases. The evaluation of automobiles is one suitable example. It is obvious that we presuppose evaluative criteria whenever we judge any particular car as good. It is equally obvious that we may choose these criteria. Anyone may say, without fear of absurdity, "Now this is what *I* mean by a good car: rack and pinion steering, disc brakes, etc." It is absurd, furthermore, to see these, or any evaluative criteria for cars, as principles to be discovered in any way analogous to the discovery of mathematical principles. We may defer on occasion to experts in the automotive field, accepting their evaluative criteria. But there is no sense in which everyone is governed by validity criteria (as in mathematics, where even the experts cannot be said to "decide" on the principles of validity), and it is perfectly sensible to establish one's own evaluative criteria—as it is not possible to do in mathematics. So the views of positivists seem clearly right in the case of automobiles.

But in legal criteria of evaluation the naturalist view seems to be a more plausible account. Legal principles cannot be decided upon by anyone who chooses to do so and still retain their status as legal principles. Consider, as a parallel to the car example, the assertion "Now this is what *I* mean by murder—a blind rage, a thoughtless killing, etc." Naturally we may all advance our own thoughts on what *ought* to count as murder. But what counts as murder is not a matter for each, or any, individual to decide. It is a given within the legal system. This point should not be misunderstood. No legal concept is immune from change, and changes in the meanings of legal concepts will ordinarily come about through the decisions of jurists. For example, though many juries will encounter only clear and indisputable cases of murder once the facts are established, some facts are not so clearly covered by the concept of murder. In deciding whether to let any borderline event count as murder a jury will be redefining the concept of murder, either in restricting the concept or in extending it to the event. But even in such cases juries are working with established criteria. They do not sit and collectively decide what the evaluative criteria are for murder, choose, in other words, the primary evaluative principles, before making the criteria-dependent evaluation of the physicalist fact. Such criteria are rather sought and discovered in the institutional fact of the law.

One does not want to push the "discovery" feature of law too far. It would be a distortion to see law as a set of immutable principles, in the Platonic sense, or even as analogous to the validity criteria of mathematics (for, unlike mathematics, the decisions of judges can remake the law). But it is also clear that the case for naturalism is more plausible where criteria-dependent evaluations occur in an established institution. No recognizable body of rules governs the evaluation of automobiles. There are no automobile schools for future car-yers, no profession of car specialists with entrance exams and ethical codes, and little in the way of precedent for criteria-dependent evaluations of cars. Though the law can logically be seen as an historical accumulation of decisions establishing evaluative criteria, the criteria must still be taken as in our experience as largely to be discovered and not decided upon anew with some primary endorsement.

2.3. Two conclusions follow from the discussion of law above.

(a) The connection between physicalist facts and institutional facts is tighter in social actions where the state of mind of the agent is sufficiently settled with institutional evidence, as in many legal contracts. The possibility of deducing *ought* from *is* is therefore stronger in cases of action occurring in terms of such institutions.

(b) The "discovery" thesis of naturalists, that primary evaluative criteria are encountered in experience, is more plausible in cases of established institutions like the law, while the positivist thesis that such criteria are results of decisions is more plausible where no well-formed institution is present.

It is important, however, not to misunderstand either naturalism or positivism on the matter of whether such discoveries or decisions really occur in fact. The positivist thesis on decisions is misconstrued if it is

thought to mean that people do endorse those arrangements, like promising, in which they hold membership. Like the social contract theories,
the thesis of a primary endorsement is not a description of some fact but
a device to justify social arrangements. Whether, for example, people do
or ever did come together to make a covenant of government is irrelevant
to the justification of authority on consent. The important thing is that
a justification of government on consent will then have important implications for the obligation of the citizen in everyday affairs. Similarly, it is
pointless to observe that people rarely, if ever, decide on primary evaluative criteria. It is still important how evaluative systems are justified, for,
as we have seen, to ground them in consent will have different implications for the obligation of the agent than a justification in terms of discovery. The point to stress about many legal contracts is that the only
evidence needed to demonstrate consent is the institutional performance
itself. Thus the basis for the positivist disjunction between *ought* and *is,*
the affirmation of the agent formed from *outside* the institutional arrangement, is set aside as irrelevant. This incorporation of the agent's
decision into the institution itself is what makes the naturalist thesis
possible, where it is not otherwise.

The hypothetical nature of a primary endorsement is not so clearly
evident in the discovery thesis informing naturalism. Plato, for example,
believed that the discovery of first principles not only does in fact occur,
but must occur in order to have a just state. (In contrast to this, both
Hobbes and Locke were prepared to allow that a state may be just even
though its origins are not in an actual social contract, occurring at some
point in time.) Still, there is also a sense in which we may say that the
discovery thesis is a device to justify social arrangements without laboring
to establish that first principles have been in fact discovered. To use legal
criteria for the concept of murder, for example, it is not necessary that
jurists go through an exercise of discovery (however that exercise may be
defined), but only that they understand that they are not free to decide
upon the criteria or establish them with a primary endorsement. The
legality (or justification) of the trial will depend upon the absence of a
decision as much as the occurrence of a discovery.

The general point, however, is that the naturalist and positivist
arguments, like most arguments, will be more or less valid as different
social arrangements are used to explicate the arguments; and the difference crucial to positivism and naturalism is the degree to which institutions are immune from criteria-establishing decisions.

3. EXTERNAL AND INTERNAL EVALUATION

Do the self-established criteria of law, not chosen but given, provide
self-evaluating principles for law? It is sometimes held that evaluative

criteria can be drawn from what a thing does. For example, the function of a kidney is to maintain the blood in a certain chemical state. We may even define the kidney in these functional terms, saying that no organ which fails to perform this function can be a kidney, and—though more extreme—any organ which performs this function is, by virtue of this performance, a kidney. Now to define a thing in terms of its function is also to provide evaluative criteria for the thing, in the sense that when we describe something as a kidney we are also saying that it performs a certain function. This is an evaluative judgment that the thing we are describing measures up to its defining function, which is what allows us to count it as the item in the first place. The evaluative criteria are internal, or self-evaluating in the sense that they are coextensive with the defining criteria.

It might be claimed that law has such defining criteria, that once we discover the function of law we will also have evaluative criteria for law which are analytic with a definition of law. Lon Fuller has advanced two versions of such a claim, each resting with varying success on the other. The first version is that a legal order must be defined evaluatively because no social arrangements count as a system of law unless they contribute to the attainment of certain moral values.[6] This claim is logically parallel to the example above, in that a certain function is taken as the essential defining feature of law, and the description of any social arrangements as a legal order is also an evaluative judgment that these social arrangements function as a means for attaining certain moral values. The second version of this claim is that law must fulfill certain procedural requirements in order to count as law.[7] Social arrangements which fail to fulfill these requirements are simply not legal systems, though it is a deficiency in Fuller's claim that no satisfactory answer is given to the question of whether anything which has the form of the defining procedures counts, by virtue of that, as a legal system. (This last point will be taken up in a moment.)

On the first version it is not always clear what the moral values are which serve as the end for the legal order, or whether any assertion for a set of moral values will elicit any broad consensus. Fuller himself recognizes that a variety of doctrines informs the concept of natural law, some overlapping and some not, and both the logical status and substantive content of the requisite moral values offered by various natural law theorists will also vary considerably. However Fuller does acknowledge a central aim common to all natural law schools, "that of discovering those principles of social order which will enable men to attain a satisfactory life

[6]Fuller, "Human Purpose and Natural Law," and "A Rejoinder to Professor Nagel," *Natural Law Forum,* Vol. 3, No. 1 (1958).
[7]Fuller, *The Morality of Law* (New Haven: Yale University Press, 1969), pp. 3–32.

in common."[8] This attempt to discover moral ends which may always deny legal status to conventional arrangements, and the concomitant assumption that such ends exist, distinguish all natural law doctrines no matter what the variation among them. The consequence of such doctrines is that, no matter what moral values are the ends which the legal order tries to attain, it is still logically possible for members of a society to claim legal status for social arrangements without these arrangements being legal on a natural law doctrine; and, further, when we describe social arrangements as a legal system we are rating the arrangements in terms of their pursuit, if not achievement, of certain moral ends.

The second version of natural law, Fuller's procedural requirements, rests on a more fleshed out definition of that which is required for law to be law. Fuller sees all law as having to fulfill the following requirements. It must (1) consist of rules, which are (2) publicized, (3) nonretroactive, (4) understandable, (5) consistent one with another, (6) feasible of execution, (7) changed only with a frequency which is tolerable to the legal subjects, and (8) congruent with their (the rules') administration.[9] Fuller argues that these requirements represent a point of fusion between law and morality, in that law to be law must embody these procedures, and these procedures are themselves minimal definitions of morality. Unlike the first version of self-evaluating principles, this second version sees law not as a means to achieve moral ends, as the kidney functions to bring about a particular chemical balance in the blood, but as the procedural embodiment of morality. On both versions, however, law is defined in terms of evaluative principles, whether ends or procedures, and so to describe a system as legal is at the same time to judge favorably on its morality, and to judge by the defining principles in terms of which the system *is* legal. In terms of the issues discussed so far, this claim means that fact and value, *is* and *ought,* are fused in a definition of law.

3.1. Though it is impossible to deny that describing something as a member of a class is an evaluation that the something has what it takes to be a member of the class, it is far from certain that such an evaluation is a *moral* evaluation. Let us, as a way of determining this, set out in a systematic way what kinds of evaluations may be a reasonable part of our experiences.

The first is a criteria-establishing evaluation. It, in turn, may be seen as directed toward defining criteria or what I will call excellence criteria. As we have seen, criteria-establishing evaluations may be in the form either of decisions or discoveries. Now setting aside for the moment Fuller's claims for law, we do have a variety of experiences where criteria

---

[8]Fuller, "A Rejoinder to Professor Nagel," p. 84.
[9]Fuller, *The Morality of Law,* (New Haven: Yale University Press, 1964), p. 39.

for saying what an item or activity is will not be synonymous with what makes it a good item or activity of that sort. Consider the example of automobiles again. To settle on what makes something a car is not yet to settle on what makes cars *good* cars, which is a different evaluation establishing excellence criteria.

The second kind of evaluation has been labeled here a criteria-dependent evaluation. It, like the criteria-establishing evaluation above, may be broken down into two types, that depending on definitional criteria and that depending on excellence criteria. The first will take the form of a judgment that a particular item counts as an instance of the defining criteria, as this thing here and now is a car. It is even possible to divide this judgment into two types, one that will be a mere classification and the other a judgment of adequacy. We may, for example, say that something is a car, but not by much. It may have four wheels, an engine, etc., but not steer well, go only ten miles per hour, break down every mile, etc. It does not realize the defining criteria of being a car to any but the most minimal extent. Another car may be a "full" or complete car, perfectly embodying what we mean a car to be. Yet we still would want to keep both these "one-of-its-kind" judgments distinct from "good-of-its-kind" judgments, the second major type of criteria-dependent evaluations. An excellent car is typically judged on the basis of criteria additional to defining criteria, usually determined by what purpose we assign to cars. Both the racing car and the family car are cars, and a car of each type may realize perfectly the defining criteria of car-ness. But what makes a racing car good, a top speed of over 200 miles per hour, road traction at racing speeds, etc., not only is not identical with what makes a family car good, high gas mileage, comfortable seating for four people, etc., but may even conflict with these criteria. The very presence of a high-speed possibility may be undesirable in a family car, and certainly the high gas consumption, restricted seating arrangements, and so on, which permit a racing car to be good are at odds with the excellence criteria for family cars. So, at least in the example of cars, we want to keep distinct "one-of-its-kind" judgments (on defining criteria) from "good-of-its-kind" judgments (on excellence criteria).

The third major type of evaluation normally found in experience is that directed at classes of items or activities. Something which is "one-of-its-kind" and even "good-of-its-kind" may yet be bad because the items or activities are themselves bad. One may, for example, judge cars, all cars as such, bad because of their effect on the environment. In such a case a car which perfectly embodies all of the defining criteria of a car may be bad precisely because of this, and rank even lower on this third criteria of evaluation than a car which just barely makes it as a car. The better the car the worse the thing called a car is, in this type of judgment.

An excellent car, "good-of-its-kind," may or may not be subject to such a judgment, for what makes a car good are criteria ordinarily distinct from what makes a car a car. Thus one may condemn cars as ruinous to man's life-needs, yet not necessarily condemn racing cars or family cars as especially responsible on the criteria which make cars either racing or family in the first place. On the other hand, we may want to judge as bad the very criteria which make cars excellent, as it is possible to say that racing is itself harmful. In either case, however, a judgment on cars as such is an external evaluation. It is a common feature of our language. We often say that people are good at what they do but what they do is liable to another judgment. The good thief and the good doctor are both good-of-a-kind, but we normally rate thieving as bad and doctoring as good.

We have, then, the following major possibilities in evaluating:

    a. criteria-establishing evaluations (discovery or decision)
        1. on defining criteria (what makes an item or activity what it is)
        2. on excellence criteria (what makes an item or activity a good instance of what it is)
    b. criteria-dependent evaluations
        1. "one-of-its-kind" (whether an item or activity realizes defining criteria)
        2. "good-of-its-kind" (whether an item or activity realizes excellence criteria)
    c. external evaluations (on items or activities themselves).

It is obvious that the third type of evaluation, external, may itself be subject to the same distinction between criteria-establishing and criteria-dependent evaluations, suggesting an infinite regress to the activity of evaluating. External evaluations are dependent on some evaluative criteria, the principles, for example, by which we say thieving is bad and doctoring is good, and these principles (and the evaluating action based on them) may be subject to another external judgment, and so on. Whether such a regress is always infinite is unlikely, for we may be prepared to accept some principles as final stopping places, something commonly the case with moral principles. But it is enough for now if we realize that the assertion of an infinite regress, even if valid, still does not deny the distinction between judgments *for* and *within* a class of items or context of activity, a and b above, and external judgments *of* a class or context, c. The possibility of asking the child's sequence of *why* questions does not mean that the sequence is an unbroken continuum. When we ask, for example, why the patient ought to have his ruptured appendix surgically removed, an answer can be given in medical terms, culminating in the observation that the operation will save the patient's life. If the inquiry is pursued further with a query as to why lives ought to be saved, then we have moved outside the context of doctoring. Additional criteria are needed from another source if the question is to be answered, or even discussed. This external quality of evaluation, the possibility of judging whole classes or contexts, is what is denoted in c, and it remains a possibility however one addresses the question of an infinite regress.

3.2. As the earlier part of this discussion demonstrated, distinctions established with one example may not be sustainable with another example. We have seen how defining criteria and excellence criteria are separable in evaluating automobiles. It is not so clear that they are separable with other things. Take doctoring as an example. We do not have, to begin with, any single defining criterion for doctoring. In an idealistic sense, we may say that doctoring is an activity whose purpose is healing. Taking just this, its purpose, as the defining criterion, the complete doctor and the good doctor are the same; for any doctor who realizes the defining criteria, who is the perfect healer, is also the doctor *par excellence.* This synthesis of "one-of-its-kind" and "good-of-its-kind" is also found in kidneys, the subject on occasion of a doctor's inquiries. The good kidney is nothing more than the kidney which performs fully the functions which define a kidney. However, unlike kidneys, doctoring is not so easily defined in terms of only purpose or function. Doctoring normally is defined in terms of rules also, which both specify the best way to heal and mark off "proper" healing from "improper" healing. The doctor of medicine will, on this basis, be distinguished from the evangelical faith-healer or the ministrations of a mother toward her child. When we introduce these additional considerations, however, a distance begins to open between "one-of-its-kind" and "good-of-its-kind" criteria. The doctor good at healing may be unorthodox in following all the rules, as we would say of any Western physician who has good results with the use of acupuncture. The doctor punctilious about the rules, on the other hand, may be poor at healing.

The claim for law which Fuller advances, in either version, seems to consist of the assertion that "one-of-its-kind," "good-of-its-kind," and external evaluations are all collapsed into a single evaluation in our conceptualization of the law. What is required for this synthesis to occur? The remarks above on doctoring suggest that one way for the first two to be reduced to one, specifically for definitional criteria to double also as excellence criteria, is for the law to be defined in terms of purpose only. If law is also defined in terms of rules, even if these rules originate as means to achieve the purpose, then logically the law could realize the rules without the purpose, as a man could be a proper doctor in terms of the rules yet not heal as effectively as the innovative—even reckless— doctor. The problem with the synthesis claim is that a definition only in terms of purpose is an inadequate account of the law, which by definition must be a body of rules whatever purpose is assigned to it. Even to talk of rule-less law is a contradiction. So it then becomes necessary to accept that the first option, a conceptualization solely in terms of purpose, is impossible. Given the necessity of rules, a legal system may then be a perfect "one-of-its-kind" in terms of the scope and rigor of its rules, its very legality, and yet not bring about moral ends (not realize "excellence" criteria) as effectively as a system less governed by rules. Such a possibility is presented here as logical, but empirical referents are not remote. It is not uncommon to say of fully developed legal systems today that law can be a hindrance to justice, when justice is defined in terms of moral purposes and law is a system of complex rules.

This distinction between rules and purposes can be overcome if we assume a necessary connection between following the rule and realizing the purpose. In math, for example, outcomes are logically dependent on method. Following the right methods leads inexorably to the right answer. In systems where such a dependence between method and outcome exists the evaluative criteria for rules and ends overlap and the conclusions above do not follow. Following the rules in math is the only way to reach the correct end. But it is difficult to see social action as a logical or mathematical system. Doctors *do* heal on occasion by breaking the rules, and legal systems *can* be impediments to justice by relying to a fault on the rules. If law were an axiomatic system, then a conceptualization in terms of purpose would not be countered by rules; but since it is not such a system some other conceptualization is required.

Another conceptualization is offered by Fuller in the second version of his claim, that certain procedures are the embodiment both of law and morality. Defining law merely in terms of procedures avoids the possibility of a conflict between rules and purposes. It thus also avoids the possibility of a legal system yielding defining ("one-of-its-kind") and excellence ("good-of-its-kind") criteria, for as social arrangements realize the defining criteria they are, *ipso facto,* good as well. There is nothing more to accomplish which will permit alternative judgments, as there are alternative judgments with the attachment of purpose.

There are, however, two problems in Fuller's procedural account. The first is that the procedures he describes do not seem to be an adequate definition of either law or morality. Many other kinds of social activity contain such procedures. Baseball, football, chess, engineering, and so on, are all dependent on procedures of the type Fuller describes. It is difficult to imagine any effective system of rules not bound by such requirements. What Fuller appears to have offered us is a description of what it is for rules to be rational, not what it means for rules to be legal or moral. Of course it might be said in support of Fuller that any rational system of rules is a point of intersection for law and morality. But this is a peculiar claim. We do normally separate the legal order from games and skills, even though we might want to say that games and skills are rule-directed activities, even lawful in some sense. Otherwise we are unable to reflect in our concepts the obvious differences between following a rule and obeying the law, breaking a rule and breaking the law, and so on in all the ways in which the law ordinarily has special status in society's systems of rules. And certainly it would be equally distorting to conceptualize morality in a way which fails to distinguish it from other rational rule systems.

Whatever the success in synthesizing defining and excellence criteria, though, it seems undeniable that the third major form of evaluation, external, is not reducible to either of the other two. Law may fulfill all of the defining and excellence criteria one postulates, yet still be challenged on external grounds. Certainly no logical contradiction occurs if we ask, is doctoring good? Is *this* legal order good? Are Fuller's procedures just? Now it is true that to question a definition of morality is to embark on a different enterprise than questioning some particular activity, something which will be discussed in the next chapter. But it is possible without complication to move to the outside of any social arrangements with an evaluative question. Like Antigone's challenge of the king, such a move is typically a moral challenge. So *any* definition of law, by virtue of the fact that law is a social convention, must be vulnerable to the possibility of external evaluation. Or, put into the language used here, both "one-of-its-kind" and "good-of-its-kind," or both synthesized as one, cannot obviate the external evaluation of the "kind" criterion itself.

This persistence of an external evaluation can be illustrated with another claim for principles of law. H. L. A. Hart has described what he calls "the minimal content of natural law." This content is the minimum which any law must observe no matter what it might assert otherwise. It consists of the assumptions of (1) human vulnerability, (2) approximate equality, (3) limited altruism, (4) limited resources, and (5) limited understanding and strength of will.[10] These assumptions are, for Hart, constraints on law which reflect the limitations of the human condition. They are, in brief, survival prerequisites, in that any society failing to incorporate them into its arrangements for living will risk destruction. But of course even survival itself is not beyond the pale of inquiry. Not only is

[10]Hart, *The Concept of Law* (Oxford: Oxford University Press, 1961), pp. 189–95.

it logically possible to ask, is survival worthwhile, but a negative answer to this question has informed the highest of our moral and religious systems in human history.

To the inquiry posed at the beginning of this section, then, the conclusion is this. Even with a definition of law which is also evaluative (though, as we have seen, there are difficulties enough with this), the external form of evaluation persists; and morality, as always statable in terms of an external evaluation, is thus not reducible to any internal criteria of evaluation.

4. SOME CONCLUSIONS

This discussion began in Chapter One with a statement of the positivist thesis on values, a thesis fundamental to the origins of modern social science. It consists, as we have seen, of the proposition that value statements do not make truth claims, and thus are not a proper concern of science, which is concerned to verify (or at least falsify) statements about experience. It is possible now to see the innocence of this thesis. It relies on a simplistic picture of language, one which (1) sees warrantability and meaning only in terms of verification, (2) relies on physicalist as opposed to institutional facts, and (3) does not take into account the performative effects of language *in use* by agents with intentions to communicate with each other. When language is freed from this narrow terrain we find that the positivist thesis on values is complicated beyond recognition. First, how a statement is verified becomes only one way to judge its meaning (for statements may have meanings prior to, and independent of, verification in a performative view of language). Second, when institutional facts are considered in terms of their distinctive qualities, *ought* and *is* are seen to be connected and separated along different dimensions than is the case in purely physicalist language. Third, the performative aspects of language provide a system for warranting propositions distinct from the verificationist system of positivist science, in that the conditions of utterance in language use can sustain evaluations and create obligations. In short, the assertion that value statements make no truth claims is an assertion dependent upon a theory of language which does not relate the whole story. Alternative theories of language supply new criteria of adequacy, especially for value propositions.

Finally, as we have seen in this chapter, viewing social phenomena as institutional facts will provide the setting for an exploration into the forms and criteria for evaluations without the crippling burden of verification requirements. In particular, we have seen that types of institutions vary in terms of their capacity to sustain the positivist *vs.* naturalistic theses, law being more prone in its reliance on tradition and rules to support naturalism. Even law, however, cannot eliminate that peculiar external quality to evaluation which we so often invoke in moral evaluation.

FOR FURTHER READING

Fuller, Lon. *The Morality of Law.* New Haven: Yale University Press, 1969.
Hart, H. L. A. *The Concept of Law.* Oxford: Oxford University Press, 1961.
Winch, Peter. *The Idea of a Social Science.* New York: Humanities Press, 1958.

MORAL EVALUATION

1. SOME PROBLEMS

Few things are so treacherous as an attempt to "define" morality. Two thousand years of moral philosophy, as variegated as a quilt, rest heavily on the definer. Some of the issues raised in this history seem impossible to reconcile. Prominent among these is the source of moral principles, whether (as we have seen) in discovery or decision, and if in discovery exactly where and how principles are to be discovered. No less important is the issue of form *vs.* substance. Can morality be defined in terms of some substantive moral principles, as "Love your neighbor"? Or must we be content with a formal account on procedural or logical grounds? Is a formal account of morality even possible? Then there is the matter of situational *vs.* universal ethics. Is morality bound to particular contexts? Can it, or should it, exceed situational constraints? Cutting across all of these issues is the thought, unsettling for the moral philosopher, that morality is nothing more than what people say it is at any given time and place; and thus morality may be catalogued by the empirical scientist, but not conceptualized by the moral philosopher unless he realizes that only *his* morality is being conceived, not necessarily anyone else's.

To thread our way through the labyrinth of issues presented above it is helpful to be modest in our goals. Obviously no single conceptualization of morality will bring together positions as different from one another as those comprising the history of moral philosophy. But two strategies do present themselves as reasonable ways to proceed. We might ask, first, what kind of moralities are required, or suggested, by the various and conflicting views on values discussed up to now. Second, we might critically examine these various moral theories to see which more adequately accounts for our ordinary use of moral language. The modesty of this task cannot be stressed enough. It will contribute almost nothing to settling on who is right and wrong in the long tradition of theorizing on moral matters. It will do little in the way of identifying what, if anything, various moral philosophers have in common. What these two strategies *will* do is allow us to judge the plausibility and usefulness of various conceptualizations of morality, even though none can be legislated out as not what morality "really" means.

The possibility that morality may mean nothing beyond what people say it means presents a different problem. To solve this problem, to deny the posssibility, requires a more exacting strategy than merely overviewing the moral field. What must be demonstrated, as a condition for this inquiry to succeed even in a modest way, is that the concept of morality contains within it definitional requirements which cannot be overlooked if it is morality we are specifying. This demonstration is more exacting in its partisanship. If definitional requirements can be demonstrated, then not just anything can be moral, either in action or language, just because people say it is. Something, formal or substantive, must constrain the range of possible definitions. We will try to discover what these limiting factors might be, for without them the present conceptual exploration is impossible.

2. EMOTIVIST MORALITY

The conventional wisdom in social science, as we have seen, is that value statements do not make truth claims. Since moral statements, whatever else they are, are a species of value statement, the social scientist will also view moral statements as noncognitivist assertions, capable of neither truth nor falsity. This effectively removes morality from positivist social inquiry. But seeing value statements as noncognitivist does not make morality totally without sense or function. It merely denies its truth.

Let's examine a typical moral assertion, "Do not kill." This assertion can be seen either as an imperative (in the way it is presented here) or as elliptical for "No one ought to kill." Though, as we shall see in a moment, there are vast differences between an imperative and an *ought* statement, a positivist will submerge any such differences to the fact of a moral statement's noncognitivism, whatever the form of the statement. The question then is, what is the function of moral assertions given that such assertions are not statements which can be verified as true or false? (The issue of whether statements which do not make truth claims are really statements is being set aside here with the use of the term "assertion.") It seems, upon inspecting the moral assertion above in conjunction with the denial that it is making a truth claim, that its function may be either (a) to express the speaker's emotions, attitudes, or state of mind, or (b) to persuade the listener to feel or act in some way, or both (a) and (b).[1]

2.1. The view of moral statements as vehicles to express emotion can be drawn from the apparent overlap between our favorable and unfavorable postures toward things and our moral judgments of them. It seems almost a contradiction to say that we are opposed to the moral thing to do, for morality appears to represent the highest of our sentiments. Thus, on this view, to utter a moral assertion is to express a favorable or unfavorable posture toward it in direct correspondence to the moral judgment expressed. In the example above, to utter the injunction against killing is to express an extreme distaste, even an abhorrence, of killing. It is not a truth claim, it being senseless to ask of an emotive expression whether it is true or false, but it is not a nonsense expression either. It is, for want of a better phrase, an emotive expression, and it has a distinct function to perform.

There is, however, one major difficulty with the emotive account of moral assertions which makes the account impossible to sustain on its own. It is that no account of exactly what is being expressed with an emotive assertion will allow moral propositions to function the way they do function in our language. In the simplest version of what is being expressed, a moral assertion in emotivism can be said to be another form of "I like (or dislike) *X.*" Aside from the offensive reduction of moral propositions to matters of taste, leaving "I like ice cream" at the same logical level as "Do not kill" or "Killing is wrong," the collapse of moral assertions to likes ignores the obvious function of morality in governing and ranking likes. Plato began moral philosophy by asking how a man can be in two volitional states at the same time, both wanting something and not wanting it. He proceeded to develop his moral philosophy around a distinction between kinds of wants, informed and uninformed, letting the former govern the latter. Thus the alcoholic who wants a drink, yet doesn't want a drink on the basis of his reasoned evaluation of what drinking does to him, will be moral by letting the want which is informed by reason govern his actions. Now to reduce moral assertions to mere likes will not provide for this legislating of likes which has seemed so fundamental to moral language as commonly understood and to moral thinking since its inception in Western history. It is, on this basis alone, a clearly inadequate formulation of moral discourse.

[1]The "expressing" function was emphasized by the early positivists, especially A. J. Ayer, *Language, Truth and Logic* (New York: Dover Publications, Inc., 1946), while the "persuasive" function was stressed by C. L. Stevenson, *Ethics and Language* (New Haven: Yale University Press, 1967).

More complex versions of what a moral assertion expresses fare no better than the simple version. Suppose we say that moral assertions express attitudes, or states of mind, something like "I approve of this" as opposed to "I like this." The immediate advantage of this complicating procedure is that it provides for a legislating of likes or wants by a more reflective evaluation. Even reflective evaluations, however, seem themselves governable by morality. We often judge attitudes, even states of mind on occasion, as moral or immoral. If moral propositions do nothing but express attitudes then, like the problem of likes, we have no way of expressing the perfectly coherent judgment that some attitudes, or states of mind, are morally good and others are morally bad. The problem with reducing moral statements to expressions of anything is that morality typically functions to legislate or rank the anything which is expressed, and it cannot do this if it is to be merely a vehicle for expressing and nothing else. The trouble is not that an adequate formulation hasn't been found for what a moral assertion may express but that moral assertions seem to have to do more than merely express if they are to be moral assertions (though they may also function to express some posture on the part of the speaker, however that posture may be defined).

2.2 At the very least, then, some other function must be allowed for moral assertions. The most common addition to the "expressing" function is the "persuasive" function. In its simplest version, this function is interpreted as the arousal of emotions, and is usually attached to the "expressing" function. Thus, the no-killing injunction can be amended to be a combination of an expression of a negative posture by the speaker and an attempt to arouse negative postures in all listeners (even the speaker, as reinforcement). To state the case as simply as possible, "X is evil" is both an expression of dislike (loathing, disapproval, etc.) and an effort to get others to dislike (loathe, disapprove, etc.) X as well.

The advantage of the persuading function is that it introduces a dimension of the governing or legislative quality of morality which the expressing function misses. It is not that we merely express our feelings or attitudes in moral discourse, but that we also want to get others to share these feelings or attitudes, even to the point of changing their behavior. Any inspection of moral language will reveal this persuading function. Typical moral propositions like "Do not kill," "Love your neighbor," "Promises ought to be kept," etc., are instruments to guide or direct others, not merely to express feelings or attitudes. Unlike the statements of science, moral statements often take the form of commands (Do X) or prescriptions (You ought to do X). It is, in fact, precisely this normative form which edges moral assertions outside empirical science, which (as we have seen) is primarily concerned with empirical and analytic statements.

Even with this advantage, however, the combination of an expressing and persuasive function still seems inadequate as an account of moral
assertions. The combined account does not, for one thing, go to the heart
of the governing or legislating issue. An account of moral assertions in
terms only of the expression function suffers, as we have seen, from the
liability of not permitting morality to govern or rank the feelings or
attitudes asserted, something morality must be able to do. If I say "Do
not kill" to someone, and he kills, obviously I will not be satisfied with
the fact that I have successfully expressed my opposition to killing. I will
want the listener not to kill, which is what the moral assertion means to
accomplish. So the persuasive function must be added to the expression
function if we are to make sense of moral propositions. But notice that
the governing function of morality is not merely persuasion, but persuasion in accordance with some evaluative principle. A moral assertion
doesn't merely *get* someone to do something. It prescribes the *proper*
course of action.

The best way to elaborate this point is to see how *persuasion* and
prescription differ. Let us state as a fundamental requirement for any
moral system that it must tell us what we ought to do. Try to imagine a
morality where this function is not performed, where only descriptive
statements are offered with no hint as to the proper or right course of
action. Such a system cannot really be considered a morality, since by
definition a morality must spell out what is moral and immoral (what to
do and what not to do). Now the "expressing" view of morality is inadequate in not permitting moral assertions to govern or rank the feelings,
attitudes, or states of mind being expressed by moral assertions. Morality
must be able to tell us which feelings, attitudes, or states of mind are
morally good, which morally bad. The "persuasive" view of morality
introduces a governing function, in that it recognizes the attempt of
moral propositions to modify thoughts and actions. But persuasion as
such, even with the expressing function, does not recognize the evaluative criteria found in all moral systems which provide for judgments of
good and bad.

Consider persuasion without moral principles of any sort. I can *get*
someone to do something in a variety of ways. I can lie, trick, force, even
point out the moral thing to do (without endorsing the moral principles
contained therein). If I succeed in modifying the behavior of the one
whom I am trying to persuade, then I have "governed" his actions,
perhaps his thoughts if I am particularly successful. But of course there
is a distinction between this, persuasion, and *moral* persuasion. To persuade morally I cannot lie or trick or force, or use moral principles
indifferently. The point to moral direction is that the *proper* course of
action is being demonstrated, perhaps even pressed upon another. And

the very evaluative criteria which mark off the proper course of action will constrain the types of things I can do to get someone to act, and specify what it is one must do in order to fulfill the moral directive. If it is merely persuasion I am engaged in, then *that* I have gotten someone to act, the outcome of my efforts alone, may be the only mark of success. In moral persuasion the outcome can never be the sole measure of success. Unlike a merely persuasive effort, a moral directive like "Love your neighbor" may stand as warranted in the face of noncompliance. Persuasion as such has failed if it fails to modify behavior. A moral assertion still points out the right course of action even if people do not follow it. The demonstration, or communication, of the moral thing to do is always part of what a moral assertion is about.

Also, there is an internal dimension to moral direction which persuasion as such cannot accommodate. If someone is gotten to do something yet is not convinced that he ought to do it, then he is not *acting* morally. He may be *behaving* morally in the sense that what he does accords with the moral norm. But no moral agency occurs. The agent can be moral only by assenting freely to the moral principle involved. We would not normally blame a man for what he has done at the point of a gun. We do not normally credit him either, for he is said not to be responsible for his actions. He is moved to action from external forces to which he has not assented. This being so, we cannot then credit a man for moral action unless he does so from conviction. This internal requirement for moral agency is not adequately covered by persuasion. Not only does persuasion, as any means to get someone to do something, include a wide range of devices which modify behavior without necessarily convincing the agent of the rightness of the action (tricks, lies, etc.), but getting someone to do something may be accomplished without any verbal utterance at all. The simple flash of a gun, without any words exchanged, may be sufficient to get the bank teller to release his cash. Subliminal advertising may communicate nothing, yet effectively alter behavior. It is obvious that such persuasive devices convince no one of anything, and thus are not variations on moral direction. The conclusion is that only some kinds of persuasion can be moral, those that rest on evaluative principles which we are willing to count as moral principles.

The fundamental problem in the persuasive interpretation of moral assertions is that the success criteria are wrong. In morality we do not ask how persuasive something is (though persuasion may be a part of moral discourse), but rather how warranted it is. An assertion may not persuade at all, yet still be a moral assertion. Conversely, an assertion may persuade effectively, yet be an amoral or even immoral proposal. So while the directive or guiding quality of moral discourse must be recognized, it is important to keep in mind that morality is concerned to tell us what we ought to do, and getting us to do it is always subordinate to the evaluative principles on which these prescriptions rest.

Finally, persuasion is normally occasioned by a lack of accord. One does not persuade another if he already shares the convictions toward which one would move him, or is already doing that which one would persuade him to do. Yet moral assertions may be uttered sensibly enough in conditions of accord. A moral assertion may stamp approval on action over which there is no disagreement or even divergent attitudes. Plato's *Republic* is often taken as a paradigmatic case of consensus politics. Yet moral evaluation is possible in the *Republic.* The Guardians may, for example, pronounce something as good by enacting it as policy. Or, in societies short of the ideal, a moral assertion may identify the moral principles toward which all ought to aspire, again with accord *not* a condition for such assertions to make sense. The capacity of moral assertions to be sensible in conditions of accord is a function of their use as instruments to praise or blame, commend or criticize, something merely persuasive utterance does not do.

2.3. The deficiencies of an emotivist morality, either in the "expressive" or "persuasive" versions, or both versions combined, are these: (1) no provision is made for the evaluative principles on which morality prescribes or judges; (2) no allowance is made for the requirements of moral agency: and (3) morality is restricted to conditions where accord is missing. Recognizing these deficiencies provides for the following requirements in any moral system. First, moral propositions must contain evaluative principles, and, second, moral assertions are prescriptive. Though there is much yet to be accomplished in "defining" morality, it appears that one major objection to this exercise has been met. If morality must be a discourse which rests on principle, and prescribes what ought to be done, then we have at least two formal principles which constrain any possible definition of morality. Or, put more directly, morality cannot be whatever anyone says it is unless what they say it is at least fulfills the principled and prescriptive requirements identified so far.

3. GOOD REASONS MORALITY

One consequence of distinguishing *prescription* (oughts) from *persuasion* (getting someone to act) is that moral assertions are revealed as propositions supervenient on reasons. An *ought* statement typically requires supporting considerations. If I tell someone that he ought to quit smoking, he is within his rights to ask me why. The dialogue proceeds rationally as I furnish reasons to support my prescription. Nothing of this sort is required in persuasion, which may not even (as we have seen) be verbal. If moral assertions are prescriptions, then like all prescriptions they rest on reasons. Notice that the supervenience of moral assertions on reasons shifts attention from the verification of moral assertions to their *rationality*. Any proposition which can be supported with reasons is a rational proposition amenable to judgments of sensibility and warrantability, not merely a truthless device to express feelings or to persuade.

3.1. A distinctive model of morality is possible on a "reasoned" view of moral assertions. One version of it, advanced by Stephen Toulmin, likens moral reasoning to scientific reasoning.[2] Toulmin sees morality in terms of function, what a moral assertion does in use, but also views morality as a rational system. For Toulmin, any discourse is characterized by its purpose and the types of considerations appropriate to support the propositions contained in the discourse. The aim of science, for example, is to give a satisfactory account of experience. A scientific statement will be more or less useful, more or less worthy, as it contributes to that purpose. The considerations which support scientific statements will be formed from the purpose of science, to render experience intelligible.

Consider for a moment how any proposition becomes a reason in the first place. Take the following propositions as sample candidates. (1) There is an exam in the morning. (2) It is raining outside. (3) The President is on vacation. Now these propositions are random statements of fact, not reasons, until we have some prescriptive statement plus a purpose. In this case, "you ought to study tonight" is supportable with proposition (1) and the aim of getting through school with grades as high as possible. The descriptive proposition stating there is an exam in the morning is a reason for action only in terms of the *ought* and the stated purpose.

The considerations which support scientific statements are not reasons for action, but still may be seen as reasons for accepting a statement of fact, a law, or a theory. Let's illustrate this point from the perspective of the statement to be supported with reasons. Archimedes' theory of displacement, "A solid will displace its own volume of a liquid when totally immersed in the liquid" is supportable with facts. The appropriate facts are descriptive statements, measures of particular results when solids are immersed in liquids. These descriptive statements can be seen as reasons for accepting, or at least not rejecting, the general theory of displacement. Other descriptive statements, say on the boiling point of water, are not supporting considerations because they are not connected

[2]Toulmin, *Reason in Ethics* (Cambridge: Cambridge University Press, 1960.)

in any way to the theory of displacement, much as statements 2 and 3 are irrelevant to the *ought* statement on studying.

Though the notion of a purpose is not so closely connected to reasons in the science example as it is in the action example above, where the *ought* directs action only with the assumption of the purpose, there is a sense in which we can see that the theoretical statement on displacement is finally sensible only as a means to account for experience. To ask *why* solids displace their own volume of a liquid in the way that they do is a nonsense question, though to ask *why* one should study even when there is an exam in the morning is a sensible query answered by the statement on purpose. But one may still chase the theoretical statement back to a purpose on a different logical level, *why* accept the statement in the first place. The answer, because it is a more useful account of experience, implies that the purpose of science is to render such an account; and this purpose will also have at least an indirect effect on what counts as a supporting consideration for scientific statements, since without the aim of explanation (as an account of experience) any kind of fact may be as appropriate a piece of evidence as any other. The scientific game, in short, is nonsense without the acceptance of explanation as its goal.

There are two implications of this view of science which should be stressed. The first is that, unlike all metaphysical philosophies and many other philosophies of science, this kind of science eschews any attempt to describe or explain reality. Scientific theories are taken only as refined maps for experience, helpful in finding our way about in experience but making no claim to have depicted either the totality of sensory experience or any part of some extramental reality. This implication follows from the notion of explanation as an account of experience, for if scientific laws and theories are seen as instruments to render experience intelligible, then they are judged as warrantable not as they describe reality but on the pragmatic criteria of how effectively they carry out the assigned purpose. A map, analogous to a scientific theory on this view, is not good or bad merely as it describes the terrain, but as it "works" in making our travels successful. So too scientific theories, on this view, are more or less useful as they give us an account of that phenomena which we take as the stuff of our experiences. This view of science has been called, appropriately enough, "instrumental," as opposed to "realistic" or "descriptive" versions of science.

The second implication is that science is self-limiting in reflective inquiry. We might, as suggested in the last chapter, direct an endless series of questions at any justification. To the stated purpose in the action example above, getting through school with grades as high as possible, it may always be asked, why get through school with grades as high as possible, and so on *ad infinitum*. Similarly, to say that a solid displaces its own volume of a liquid when immersed in the liquid may itself be subject to questions about how such an occurrence is possible, or how the explanation of the occurrence is itself justified. Now Toulmin claims that in science one can reach a point where such questions exceed the recognizable boundaries of science, and thus on scientific terms are meaningless. If, after a full graphic or conceptual explanation of immersed solids in liquids, a questioner still asks how such an event is possible, or for a justification of the explanation itself, then he may be asking questions science cannot answer. Such inquiry leads into an area which is beyond the scope of scientific inquiry. Toulmin refers to the question of whether light is *really* a wave or a particle. Such a question is unanswerable by current forms of scientific inquiry. It is enough to know that sometimes light is viewed as a wave, other times as a particle. What it is *really* cannot be answered by scientists, nor is an answer required in order to do science. The instrumental character of science, in short, rules out any authoritative statement on reality, or ultimate justification of explanations. Science is an enterprise limited in its capacity to provide answers. These limitations are drawn by the purpose and rules with which we identify science as a distinctive activity.

Ethics (or moral reasoning) is, for Toulmin, similar in form to scientific discourse. It is, first, a rational activity in the sense that ethical propositions are supportable with reasons. It should be noticed again that this view of both science and ethics deflects the positivist thesis on verification. In this, Toulmin's view, the verification of statements as true or false is irrelevant. What is important is how statements are warranted with the use of supporting reasons. The difference between a "good reasons" philosophy of adequacy and a verificationist philosophy can be illustrated as follows. To the verificationist, the statement "President Nixon is 60 years old" is a proposition to be proved true or false as it conforms to experience. The "good reasons" philosopher will see the statement as a warranted assertion as evidence is brought to bear in support of it. No appreciable difference separates the two positions on such a statement. But now consider the statement "Matter is soluble." Since this statement attributes a disposition to matter to perform in certain ways under certain conditions, and these conditions can never be exhausted, then the verificationist is stuck with a statement which is not verifiable. The "good reasons" philosopher, on the other hand, will be content to see dispositional statements as more or less warranted in terms of the evidence at hand. No dilemma is presented with a dispositional because truth or falsity is not at issue. Now consider the statement "All men ought to love their neighbor." To the verificationist, this statement is meaningless because we have no means of verifying it. But the "good reasons" philosopher will, again, be able to accept the statement as more or less warranted on the basis of supporting considerations, for example that following such a prescription will make for more congenial zoning policies, and so on. A "good reasons" view of adequacy, then, escapes the verificationist critique of evaluative statements by replacing verification with the notion of supporting reasons. Value statements become analogous to advice, which can be weighed as worthy or unworthy (though not true or false) through rational discussion.

It remains true, however, that the reasons supporting a moral assertion may themselves be questioned, as the consideration of more congenial zoning policies above may be queried as to worthiness. Why is a more congenial zoning policy morally good, it may be asked, and any reason advanced as an answer to *that* question may be subject also to an evaluative inquiry. In answer to this, Toulmin suggests that, like science, moral inquiry has its limits beyond which inquiry becomes senseless. Suppose, for example, that I say "Joan, you ought to return the book to Jones," and Joan asks why. Then I say, "Because you promised to," which is a perfectly good reason for carrying out the *ought* I have stated. Now if Joan then asks "Why ought I to keep promises?" she has, according to Toulmin, moved outside the ethical game of promising. It is a question roughly equivalent in science to, what is light *really,* a wave or a particle? If Joan persists in her questioning, she may also move outside of the game of ethics as such. A questioner of science who presses back to the goal of science, explanation, and then questions the goal, is at that point engaged in an inquiry external to science. There is also, for Toulmin, a goal for ethics. It is social harmony. Though this goal is not as solidly entrenched as the goal of explanation is for science, Toulmin maintains that we normally view ethics as aiming at bringing individual wills into a harmonious state. Thus, in the inquiry above, if promising is justified as an instrument for social harmony, and *this* reason, social harmony, is questioned as to worthiness, then the questioner has moved outside conventional ethics. The infinite regress of questioning is halted in the same way it is halted in science, by an identification of the purpose and rules of ethical inquiry and a further assumption that the purpose and rules of ethics mark off a form of activity which has its own limits to requests for justification.

Toulmin also maintains that a "good reasons" view of moral discourse will provide for a connection between *ought* and *is* which does not require the endorsement of a primary ought. Ethical evaluation, for Toulmin, takes place within a system of rules (as does scientific explanation). An *ought* statement, like "You ought to return the book," is supportable with reasons (facts) in accordance with the conventional rules of the promising game linking the ought to certain facts. Conversely, from a description of conditions within evaluative systems, Joan borrowing the book, promising to return it, and so forth, it becomes reasonable to infer that Joan ought to return the book. Like Searle's claim, discussed in Chapter Two, descriptive statements are sufficient to establish an *ought.* Unlike Searle's claim, the establishment is not necessarily a deduction, but only a warranted inference from facts which function as reasons to support the *ought.*

3.2. Though Toulmin's escape from the conundrums of verification is reasonable, the "good reasons" system of morality seems deficient in two important respects. The first is that the reliance on a system of rules, with a purpose, does not in itself avoid the necessity of endorsing a primary *ought.* It has been pointed out that Toulmin's version of ethics merely moves the *ought* from the premises to the rules of inference.[3] By this is meant that while the primary *ought* is not endorsed within the evaluative system, the inferential rules which permit the conclusion of an *ought* must be endorsed before the *ought* can be legitimately inferred. This criticism was made earlier of Searle's derivation, where the agent who promises must endorse the promising game or the promise is not authentic. So, too, in science, the fundamental imperative of explanation must be accepted in order for science to be conducted rationally.

There *is* a case which can be made against the requirement of a primary *ought.* It relies on ethics as a system of rules, but it elevates the system of rules to a state of natural necessity impossible to accommodate in Toulmin's instrumental philosophy. Consider the following narrative. "A man emerges from a house early in the morning dressed obviously for work. It is a cold morning. He gets into his car and turns the ignition key. The motor turns over but will not start." Given certain additional statements on the make of car and what has worked in the past in starting it, the described situation may be said to elicit the prescription, "The man ought to try the choke." The descriptive statements, strung out with sufficient length and care, may even demand the *ought.* Or, put another way, a description may reveal a need or lack which can only be filled with an *ought.* Now the positivist may want to say that we are not required to furnish that *ought.* But the naturalist will counter with the claim that the *ought* can be denied only by denying the described situation. It is obvious that, as has been pointed out on many occasions earlier in this discussion, the cogency of each opposing claim will depend on whether such descriptions represent forms of experience which cannot be rejected, which are natural entailments of the world as we know it. We have already explored

---

[3]Hare makes this point in his review of Toulmin's *Reason in Ethics* in *Philosophical Quarterly* (1950–1951), p. 372, and in his (Hare's) *The Language of Morals* (Oxford: Oxford University Press, 1964), pp. 44–46.

the possibility that law presents certain experiential requirements. It is enough to observe here that Toulmin's instrumental system of rules will not counter the positivist arguments for a primary *ought*. Only a naturalistic case for requirements in experience, and language, will permit the derivation of an *ought* without an endorsement.

The second deficiency in "good reasons" morality is in the idea of a self-limiting factor to ethical inquiry. There is a sense in which science cannot sustain questions of justification beyond a certain point. To ask, is explanation justifiable, is to ask a question which simply cannot be answered scientifically. It is outside scientific inquiry. But one can ask, should promises be kept, is social harmony worthwhile, without straining ethical discourse out of shape. Any ethical principle or any goal advanced for ethics may be evaluated ethically. Toulmin seems to recognize this with the tentative status he assigns to social harmony, leaving it as merely a conventional goal challengeable from outside convention. If it is challengeable from the outside, however, then ethics is not self-limited, and we are owed an explanation of why social harmony is even a tentative or conventional goal. Conflict, after all, is judged more valuable than harmony in some social theories.

This "open" quality to ethics, where no closed system of rules can ever pin it down, can be demonstrated in two other ways. First, unlike a scientific dispute, an ethical dispute can occur *between* systems. Two people operating in mutually exclusive rule systems can still pose moral issues for each other in the way they act. A murderer is still a moral problem for the victim even though he shares no common intellectual ground with him. Two scientists in mutually exclusive rule systems have no scientific issues or problems between them, for science is a system-dependent activity. The reason for this difference in system-dependence is very simple. Ethics is concerned with how we act, science with how we explain experience. Actions can occur, and conflict, without a common paradigm. Explanation, on the other hand, is impossible without some sharing of premises and rules (for otherwise what a warranted inference is and what counts as evidence goes unanswered).

Second, morality commonly functions to rank and evaluate kinds of activity. The good thief and the good doctor may be alike in being good-of-a-kind (see Chapter Three), but we rank doctoring as better than stealing on an external basis. This ranking is typically the result of a moral judgment. Science offers no criteria for the evaluation of activities outside of science. The salient mark of moral discourse is that it seems to have no boundaries by which an outside can be identified. Anything may be subject to moral judgment, with nothing more encompassing than moral criteria (as morality embraces thieving, doctoring, even science, in the evaluation of activities); and to see morality as a defined activity vulnerable to external evaluation seems almost contradictory.

What can be extracted from these remarks to add to our conception of morality? One feature which appears to be a requirement in any morality is an external quality. Unlike self-limiting systems like science, moral discourse is always itself fair game for questions aimed at justification. It is also a system, if it is a system at all, with the capacity to be "outside" all other systems, including morality itself. So the concept of morality, with this feature of externality added to the two features drawn from the discussion of emotivist morality, now looks like this. Moral discourse is (1) prescriptive, (2) principled (moral action and judgment rest on evaluative principles), and (3) external in form. By "external in form" is meant (a) open-textured in the sense of not limiting reflective inquiries into justification, and (b) capable of evaluating all other modes of activity without restriction.

4. UNIVERSALIZABILITY IN MORALS

Another version of "reasoned" morality is that developed by R. M. Hare.[4] Unlike Toulmin, Hare sees a sharp distinction between the form of a moral assertion and its function. What, for Hare, distinguishes moral assertions is not some peculiar function they perform, as expressing feeling, causing feeling, or bringing about social harmony, but their supervenience on reasons. Toulmin is prepared to allow that moral assertions are supportable with reasons, but still identifies their defining features in what they *do* rather than in their meaning or logical form. For Hare the important feature of a moral assertion is its form. The supervenience of a moral assertion on reasons provides for a formal definition of morality, in Hare's philosophy, for reasons are the source of a moral assertion's critical defining property: its universalizability.

4.1. To understand what this feature is it may be helpful to have some idea of what it is *not*. We may identify three primary ethical philosophies, two of which have been discussed here. One, *naturalism,* maintains (as we have seen) that value statements make truth claims. This can be disputed on two grounds: (a) value statements do not seem verifiable either analytically or empirically (see Chapter One), and (b) to view value statements as facts of any sort is, as Hare points out, to deny that which value statements do by definition, which is to evaluate. For example, if I say that "courage" is X, Y, Z facts, then I cannot use the term "courage" to commend X, Y, Z facts, which seems to be the type of thing which value terms must do if they are to be evaluative. Only by *not* reducing value language to factual language is it possible to use value terms to evaluate facts.

---

[4]Hare, *The Language of Morals,* and *Freedom and Reason* (New York: Oxford University Press, 1965).

The second major theory in ethical philosophy has been called in this discussion *emotivism*. We have seen the difficulties involved with this account of morality. To say that value assertions express something and-/or cause others to feel something is still not to capture the prescriptive quality of morality, its capacity to guide or direct action. So both naturalism and emotivism, for different reasons, fail to account for what may be the distinctive feature of moral discourse, its evaluative strength (commendation, guidance, direction, and so on). Emotivism, unlike naturalism, also fails to provide criteria for saying that one value statement is any better than any other, something we also expect moral discourse to do. Taking emotivism strictly, we cannot say which value statements are better or more warranted, certainly not which are true and which are false, but only which are better at expressing emotions and/or which are more persuasive. Given the fact that moral language seems to be used for such evaluation, any moral theory is deficient if it fails to account for this use.

Naturalism does provide evaluative criteria, the truth or falsity of value statements as they accord with publicly observable states of affairs, but at the expense of the evaluative function. We can in principle evaluate value statements as true or false with a naturalistic thesis (though what the status of *this* evaluative judgment is remains unclear), but the value statement being evaluated cannot then evaluate. To illustrate: The proposition "Courage is X, Y, Z facts" may, in a naturalistic moral philosophy, be said to be true. It is then a proposition preferable to false assertions like "Courage is A, B, C facts." If we allow the reasonable assumption that a true statement is in some way better than a false statement, precisely because it is true, then the X, Y, Z courage assertion is better than the A, B, C courage assertion. But then, as pointed out above, we cannot use the term "courage" to evaluate X, Y, Z facts, for the term *is* this set of facts. On the other hand, if we interpret "Courage is X, Y, Z facts" in an emotivist way and say the proposition merely expresses a *liking* for X, Y, Z facts and/or an attempt to *get* others to like X, Y, Z facts, then we have no evaluative criteria for saying that *this* proposition on courage is better than any other. One assertion is merely a more effective vehicle for expression, or more persuasive, than another.

The third major ethical philosophy (not discussed explicitly up to now) is known as *intuitionism*.[5] It is a form of value cognitivism, meaning that those holding to this philosophy maintain that value statements do make truth claims. Unlike naturalists, however, intuitionists do not claim

---

[5]The most famous contemporary exponent of intuitionism is G. E. Moore, "The Indefinability of Good," in *Readings in Ethical Theory* (New York: Appleton-Century-Crofts, 1970), ed. by Wilfrid Sellars and John Hospers, pp. 31–53

that value statements are varifiable like facts, as they accord with publicly observable states of affairs, but rather as they accord with certain nonobservable states of affairs. Values, in intuitionism, have been called "nonnatural" facts. A value statement is true as it corresponds to experiences which can only be intuitively perceived. In certainly the most famous case argued for intuitionism, Plato in the *Republic* argued that the highest form, the Form of the Good, is accessible only to a few on the basis of intuitive insight. This Form is a truth which must be grasped, directly and without demonstration or explanation, for it cannot be expressed in language. The important thing to notice about intuitive truth is that it is still a truth, not an emotive expression, though it is a truth which cannot be *publicly* verified.

Though intuitionism is distinct from emotivism in allowing truth content to value statements (cognitivism) while emotivism denies truth content to value statements (noncognitivism), intuitionism is similar to emotivism in not providing adequate evaluative criteria for warranting value statements. This may seem an odd claim to make in view of the fact that intuitive truth is still truth, thus seeming to provide for a ranking of evaluative statements as true or false. But when we examine how truth is determined, and thus how statements are ranked, the deficiency in evaluative criteria is easily perceived. Suppose party A has an intuitive experience which he claims establishes proposition X. Now suppose another party, B, has an intuitive experience which he claims establishes the truth of proposition Y, which is contrary to proposition X. How can the rival claims be adjudicated to arrive at the "real" truth (either X or Y or some other propositon C, since as contraries X and Y cannot both be true)? It is obvious that on an intuitive interpretation of truth no means are available to adjudicate the rival claims, since what is required for the adjudication are *public* criteria of truth. Without such criteria we simply cannot say which of the claimants is right, which wrong, since an intuitive experience by definition is fugitive to assessments of authenticity by those who do not have the critical experience.

4.2. How does Hare's moral philosophy fit into the three major philosophies identified above? The first contribution Hare makes is in recognizing, in contrast to naturalism, that value language is evaluative or prescriptive. The term "courage" may have a factual content, say certain experiences which we recognize as instances of courage (giving up one's life for another, etc.), but it also is an evaluative word. When we use it we mean to commend that which we describe as courageous. The exact relationship between the evaluative and factual content of such evaluative terms has been discussed in many ways in the first three chapters here, especially whether they are necessarily connected or are independent of one another. Hare's position is that facts and values are not necessarily connected. But the important point here is that only by allowing the duality of content in second order value terms like "courage" can the evaluative function of value language be preserved. A similar strategy supports the prescriptive quality of moral language. If we accept the strictures of either naturalism or emotivism, then we define out the obvious fact that morality tells us what we ought to do. For this reason, Hare accepts a prescriptive feature for moral discourse.

The most important contribution Hare makes, however, is the development of the "reasoned" quality of moral discourse. Both emotivism and intuitionism, as we have seen, do not give us evaluative criteria adequate to adjudicate rival claims for moral action. If we ask an emotivist what the moral course of action is, he can merely tell us his own feelings (which, on the emotivist thesis, have no more validity than the feelings of anyone else) or try to persuade us of something to which he can attach no validity. If we ask an intuitionist what the moral course of action is, he can give us the "right" answer, but he cannot defend or justify it. He can merely tell us what we ought to do, period, and we must take it or leave it on faith. The issue here is one fundamental to morality. Can moral philosophy provide us with an account of morality which will allow us not only to answer the question vital to any moral inquiry, what ought I to do, but also why ought I to do it?

Hare's attempt to answer this double question is what makes his moral philosophy distinct from the three major philosophies outlined above, and distinct from the "good reasons" thesis examined earlier. Hare, as with Toulmin, views moral assertions as supervenient on reasons. This reliance on reasons is what, for both moral philosophers, makes moral discourse rational. But Hare goes further. He sees in the notion of a reason the source of morality's universalizability. Consider for a moment what it is to give a reason for action. Let us say that I tell Smith, "You ought to spend more time with your children" and Smith, a curious sort, asks why. "Because," I say, "children do not develop well psychologically when the father is away so much." Now if this is a valid reason for Smith spending more time with his children, meaning that it is a true statement which is an appropriate support for the *ought* on some acceptable system of rules and inference, then it is also a reason for any father similar to Smith in the relevant respects to spend more time with his children. Reasons, if they are valid anywhere, are valid in all relevantly similar circumstances, meaning they are universalizable.

Naturally there are numerous ways that other fathers can be unlike Smith. But the prescription for spending more time with one's children cannot be set aside on the basis of differences which are irrelevant. The fact that Smith lives in the country and someone else, Jones, lives in the city will not be a relevant difference between the two on this issue. If, however, Jones can be home with his children only by giving up his job, and the children will be more severely deprived of emotional *and* physical security as a result, then the prescription is normally set aside by the difference. The reason is still valid which supports the prescription. It is merely that the situation is relevantly unlike the situation for which the reason establishes the prescription.

It is sometimes thought that anything can count as a relevant dissimilarity, and thus as an exception, in the sense that nothing logically rules out any criteria of relevance. If, in the example above, I want to count living in the city as a relevant exception to the prescription on spending time with one's children, then there is nothing to prevent me from doing so. Though there is much that can be included in the category of exceptions, there are two formal principles which do restrict the range of claims which legitimately can count as an exception. The first principle is that the reason for the exception be somehow relevant to the prescription. Keeping a job to maintain family security *is* relevant to the prescription on the psychological welfare of children, while living in the city does not seem to be. For residence to be relevant, some connection must be established between the substance of the prescription and residence. Otherwise the claim is nonsense. The second principle is that what is claimed as an exception cannot be reiterable to everyone else.[6] If I claim as an exception, say, to paying taxes that my house is white, then so too can everyone else claim exception on the basis of the color of their house, and if everyone is an exception in this case then we have no prescribing rule. It should be noticed that the restriction against reiterability does not apply to every prescription. Everyone can be an exception to the prescription on spending time with children if everyone is in the kind of economic situation described by the exception; and the prescription may still stand as binding where experience is otherwise. On the other hand, not everyone can be an exception to taxpaying prescriptions without a collapse of the prescription. Something particular to individual cases, not reiterable to everyone else, must be demonstrated for the exception. However, both principles, relevance and nonreiterability, do logically restrict what can count as an exception, even if (as suggested in the earlier analysis of Searle in Chapter Two) a substantive moral principle is needed to justify the exception.

The importance of a reason's universalizability, for Hare, is that it establishes restraints on moral reasoning which are purely formal in nature. It means that one cannot make an exception in moral reasoning for oneself, or anyone else, without demonstrating relevant dissimilarity.

[6]Marcus Singer makes this point in *Generalization in Ethics* (London: Eyre & Spottiswoode, 1963), pp. 87–90.

This demonstration, in turn, can be restricted logically by the requirements of relevance and, on occasion, nonreiterability. Restraint in Hare's moral philosophy, however, does not rest on these two requirements. Rather he develops the thought that some differences are accidental, and revealing this fact in conjunction with the thesis of universalizability will be a persuasive device in moral argument. In his famous description of a liberal–Nazi exchange, Hare has the liberal pointing out that if the Nazi were somehow a Jew (with the concomitant thought that only the accident of birth prevents this) then Fascist policies will also, on the thesis of universalizability, apply to him. Unfortunately, however, Hare has no answer to the Nazi who accedes to the consequences of universalizability, except for the weak empirical assertion that such fanatics are few in number. The formal requirement in moral reasoning remains, however. A moral prescription is universalizable, binding all relevantly similar individuals on the basis of its supervenience on reasons; and while fanatics escape its logical net the universalizability thesis still rules out the moral abandon of treating like cases in unlike fashion.

4.3. Hare offers the following account of morality, then, for the two questions posed earlier. Morality is statable in the form of prescriptive language, thus telling us what we ought to do. It is supervenient on reasons, thus telling us why we ought to do what we ought to do. Finally, the logic of reasons confers on moral discourse a universalizable quality removing it decisively from the personal whims of any particular person. To be moral is to be bound by a logical rule which requires everyone relevantly similar to be bound by the same moral principle as well. Morality is thus both rational (supervenient on reasons) and universalizable (prescriptive for all relevantly similar persons). With Hare we have come, obviously, a considerable distance from the early positivist thesis on values, even though Hare still accepts a noncognitivist thesis that primary evaluative statements are matters of choice, not verifiable as true or false.

Unfortunately the trip is not without some costs as well. Among these is the status of the universalizability thesis in Hare's moral philosophy. To be universalizable a moral principle must presuppose criteria of sameness by which some things are relevantly similar and others are relevantly dissimilar. But sameness criteria are not given as ontological principles. They are system-dependent. What will count as the same in one set of symbols will not necessarily count for sameness in another. This same dependence on a system can also be observed about reasons. A reason for action depends, as we have seen, on some notion of relevance by which the statement advanced as a reason can be connected to the prescription. Relevance, however, will obviously depend upon rules of inference and evidence, which may themselves differ from one system to another.

The simplest illustration of the system-dependence nature of sameness criteria and supporting reasons is in the differences between systems of proof in law and science. Two cases of murder, one by shooting, the other by poisoning, may be the same under the law but radically different as far as the scientist is concerned. Each system, law and science, will have different criteria for counting things as the same. Similarly, what constitutes proof in each system will differ. Evidence valid on scientific grounds may be invalid on legal grounds, as information secured through unauthorized wiretaps. Inferences denied in the courtroom, as a witness drawing a conclusion, may be permitted in scientific explanation. The presumption of innocence until proven guilty is missing in science, where any possible outcome may be given equal weight with any other. Naturally there are overlaps between law and science. But the point is that sameness criteria and supporting reasons are not independent of systems of rules, but in fact logically reliant on them.

If the very devices on which the thesis of universalizability is defined are system-dependent, then so too is the thesis. The consequence of this is that the thesis then becomes a thesis on rationality with no special claims to distinguish moral discourse. If, say, a doctor recommends to a patient that he ought to have his appendix taken out, and his supporting reason is that the patient has appendicitis, then of course he will be bound to accept that any relevantly similar patient, i. e., with appendicitis, ought also to have his appendix out. It is only rational that the doctor accede to the logical requirement that his reasons, and thus his prescription, be universalizable. But nothing *moral* has been effected, though morality may also be bound by rational requirements. We are left without any identifying feature of morality, though we have a cogent definition of rationality. Unfortunately, however, both doctors and murderers can be rational, each in their own way in their own systems, and only morality can separate them for judgment.

One way to maintain the special rationality of moral discourse is to view moral prescriptions as *universal,* not universalizable. By this it is meant that moral prescriptions may be distinguished by an absence of particulars in the prescription. The doctor recommending an appendix operation to his patient is making a particular recommendation to a particular patient, which then rationally must apply to that particular class of patients who evidence relevantly similar symptoms. A moral prescription, on the other hand, will often not contain particulars at all, as "No one ought to kill," or "Promises ought to be kept." These are prescriptions for men *qua* men, not for particular classes of men. Viewing moral prescriptions as universals will provide us with another feature distinctive of moral discourse, for with the concept of universality moral reasoning is distinguished from reasoning as such, something not accomplished by the universalizability thesis. A word of caution must be stressed, however. Many moral principles in ordinary language *do* contain particulars, as obligations for, say, fathers are often considered moral, yet are statements for a class of men and not all men everywhere. So relying on the concept of universality, unlike the other concepts identified earlier, is also to legislate language to some degree, a price that may be worth the accommodation with the obvious universality of many of our important moral principles.

5. THE CONCEPT OF MORALITY

At the beginning of this chapter we set out to "define" morality. Our task was informed by a range of contributions in moral philosophy and an appeal to moral language. From the critical exploration of a number of moral philosophies, the following conceptual outline of morality emerges.

   a. prescription: morality as a guide or directive for action
   b. evaluative principles: morality as a system for ranking and judging
   c. external in form: morality as open-textured and with unrestricted evaluative capability
   d. universal: moral prescriptions as containing no particulars

The first thing which can be said about this set of concepts is that it is a *formal* definition of morality. The immediate disadvantage of this is that nothing then can rule out the fanatic. The prescription, "Everyone ought to kill one another" is as congenial with this system of morality as the prescription "Everyone ought to love one another." The immediate advantage, on the other hand, is that the definition does not require a choice of one of these two contrary principles. Given the well-known variance in moral codes, any attempt to say some principles are right, others wrong, is to move from philosophy to partisanship. The cost in short, of formality is the moral rationality of fanaticism, though at the bargain price of setting out certain necessary requirements which all moralities must fulfill in order to be moralities.

The second, and last, thing to be said about the morality defined here is that it is not definitive. A situational moral philosopher, like Sartre, will dismiss this set of concepts as irrelevant to moral action, which he sees as always authentic only in particular contexts. Also, the moral philosopher (or moralist) who insists on some substantive content to morality in the face of differing moral codes will be far from satisfied with what has been accomplished in this chapter. It is obvious that the strategy adopted here has not been to rule out the alternative ways to define morality suggested by the questions opening this chapter, as to build a case for the justification of the particular conceptualization of morality developed here. If the justification is unconvincing, then the supporters of alternative definitions will go away unnourished intellectually. But, on the other hand, the concepts extracted here from a variety of moral philosophies comprise at the least a plausible version of morality. Instead of shouting about morality and society with no conception of what morality means, the discussion here can now proceed into issues of social morality armed with at least a reasonably defensible specification of that key troublesome term, "morality."

FOR FURTHER READING

Castenada, H. N., and Nakhnikian, G., eds. *Morality and the Language of Conduct.* (Detroit: Wayne State University Press, 1965).

Frankena, William. *Ethics.* Englewood Cliffs, N. J.: Prentice-Hall, Inc., 1963.

Hare, R. M. *Freedom and Reason.* New York: Oxford University Press, 1965.

——— *The Language of Morals.* New York: Oxford University Press, 1964.

MacIntyre, Alasdair. *A Short History of Ethics.* New York: The Macmillan Company, 1966.

Meldon, A. I., ed. *Essays in Moral Philosophy.* Seattle: University of Washington Press, 1958.

——— *Rights and Right Conduct.* New York: Humanities Press, 1970.

Moore, G. E. *Principia Ethica.* Cambridge: Cambridge University Press, 1962.

Oppenheim, Felix. *Moral Principles in Political Philosophy.* New York: Random House, Inc., 1968.

Sellars, Wilfrid, and Hospers, John, eds. *Readings in Ethical Theory.* 2nd ed. New York: Appleton-Century-Crofts, 1970.

Singer, Marcus. *Generalization in Ethics.* London: Eyre & Spottiswoode, 1963.

Stevenson, Charles. *Ethics and Language.* New Haven: Yale University Press, 1967.

Toulmin, Stephen. *Reason in Ethics.* Cambridge: Cambridge University Press, 1960.

Wallace, G., and Walker, A. D. M., eds. *The Definition of Morality.* New York: Barnes and Noble, 1970.

CHAPTER FIVE

MORALITY AND SOCIETY

1. THE ENFORCEMENT OF MORALS

One of the more obvious issues in the field of social morality is whether law should be an instrument to enforce morals. Not only is this issue rich with theoretical implications, but positions staked out on it affect us daily. If the government assumes the role of moral protector, whatever is included in the term "morals," it can scarcely be doubted that life will be different than if the government is legally indifferent on moral matters. Only the briefest of considerations on what moral codes might require, principles on taking life, paying debts, sexual practices, familial responsibilities, and how society will differ as the government regulates or abstains from regulating such activities is sufficient to see how important the issue of enforcement is. The difference between the political theories of Aristotle and Hobbes turns substantially on this issue: Aristotle's state promotes the moral welfare of its citizens while Hobbes' state is silent on matters of citizen morality.

In September 1957, the Wolfenden Committee of Great Britain issued a report recommending that homosexual practices between consenting adults should no longer be a crime. In supporting this recommendation the Committee set out its views on the general function of law in society. Law, according to the Committee, (a) preserves public order and decency, (b) protects the citizen from what is offensive or injurious, and (c) prevents the exploitation or corruption of others, particularly the young, weak, inexperienced, or dependent.[1] This being the general

---

[1]Wolfenden Report, Report of the Committee on Homosexual Offenses and Prostitution, 1957, Cmd. 247. Cited as "Wolfenden."

function of law, it follows that society ought not to intrude in matters of private morality, where the individual ought to have freedom of choice and freedom to act without the constraints of law; for nothing in the function of law warrants such an intrusion.

One of the most important arguments against the views expressed by the Wolfenden Committee is advanced by Patrick Devlin.[2] Devlin argues that society ought to enforce morals, both because of the nature of law and the nature of morals. Several things can be said of the Wolfenden Report before examining Devlin's case, all of them pointed out by Devlin as a preface to his argument. First, *public* morality is not excluded from regulation. Only private morality, as in sexual behavior between consenting adults, is removed from the law's jurisdiction. This immediately places a burden on the Wolfenden Report's supporters to establish a general distinction between private and public morality if the Report's arguments are to be sustained. Second, it should be noticed that, as a factual matter, law is often justified by reference to morality. Laws against murder, for example, are frequently defended on the grounds that unwarranted killing is morally wrong. The rightness or wrongness of such justifications has yet to be explored in this discussion. But it is worth noting that the general conclusion of the Wolfenden Report, that private morality should be independent of the law, ought not to obscure the fact that law and morals are commonly intertwined. Third, while consent is vital to morality, it is not always relevant to law. Murder between consenting adults is still prohibited by law, even though it is not technically a menace to others and may be considered "private" or any criteria used to categorize some moral issues as private. So the simple fact of consent and privacy in moral actions is not in itself sufficient to exclude regulation by law. There must be something else about some moral action which justifies its independence from law if the Wolfenden Committee's report is to be plausible.

The main part of Devlin's argument against the Wolfenden Report can be summed up as answers to the three questions Devlin poses for his inquiry. There are as follows:

1. Has society the right to pass judgment at all on matters of morals? Ought there, in other words, to be a public morality, or are morals always a matter for private judgment?
2. If society has the right to pass judgment, has it also the right to use the weapon of the law to enforce it?
3. If so, ought it to use that weapon in all cases or only in some; and if only in some, on what principles should it distinguish?[3]

[2]Devlin, *The Enforcement of Morals* (New York: Oxford University Press, 1970).
[3]Devlin, *The Enforcement of Morals,* pp. 7–8.

Devlin maintains that there is a public morality. His case rests on a view of society as a community of ideas. The fact of an aggregate, people merely living together, is not for Devlin sufficient to explain a society. Some fundamental agreement among the members of a society furnishes the cohesion without which societies cannot exist. Further, ethics must be a part of this community of ideas. Nothing is more fundamental than convictions on what is good and evil, and so an absence of consensus in morality will be an absence of consensus on the most fundamental ideas in a society. It follows, for Devlin, that a recognized morality is necessary to the existence of society. This being so, a society is not only warranted in regulating morality, but it is impelled by the necessity of preserving itself to intrude in moral matters.

So Devlin's answer to the first question posed above is an unequivocal *yes*. His support for this answer is comprised of three assertions. First, there is the empirical claim that society cannot exist without a fundamental agreement on morals. Second, there is the evaluative claim that a society is warranted in preserving itself. Third, there is the deduction from these two statements that a society is warranted in regulating morals. For Devlin it follows quickly that the law is the proper instrument for regulating behavior. To do something legally is already, as suggested earlier, to justify what one is doing. So the assertions on survival and morals provide the grounds for regulation, and the self-justifying nature of law supports its use as the means for regulation. The answer to the second question is also a yes.

Buttressing the answers to the first two questions is Devlin's view that immoral action weakens the individual and thus eventually the society in which he lives. A society of drunks is obviously deficient. For Devlin a society of immoral individuals is also deficient. This deficiency is not a consequence of the fact that society requires a consensus on morality in order to exist, but rather is a result of immoral action itself. To act immorally is, for Devlin, to be somehow worse off than acting morally. Now if this point about morality is conceded, then no distinction is possible between private and public morality. All immoral action, even between consenting adults, becomes an exploitation of human weakness. Not only does this then allow morality to be regulated by law according to the Wolfenden Report, but it also permits the regulation of morals on still other grounds covered by Devlin's premise on survival. If a society is warranted in maintaining itself, then it may regulate the needed consensus on morals *and* regulate also the behavior of its members on the principles of morality contained in the moral consensus. Not only must people agree on moral matters, but also they must act morally as defined by this agreement; and in both cases the maintenance of the society is the premise for the regulation.

If all immoral action is considered as an exploitation of human weakness, it also follows that no field of morality is excluded from legal regulation. Particular cases may be excluded from coverage by the law, but no theoretical limits to the use of law can be set. Every moral issue is a candidate for regulation by virtue of the vital connections accepted by Devlin between morality and the survival of a society. Or, put differently, a society may regulate any moral issue it decides to regulate as the issue is judged to be vitally connected to the survival of the society. The only principles which Devlin allows may affect such regulation are elastic principles for balancing private and public interest. One will want to maximize individual freedom consistent with the integrity of society, or respect privacy as much as possible. But these are not restraining principles. They are considerations to be taken into account when society is regulating morals. Devlin maintains that protecting the individual is not a sufficient goal of the law. Law must also protect society, which is the warrant for the legal enforcement of morals.

Anyone arguing the enforcement of morals is obligated to give an account of morals, and Devlin supplies one. The moral judgments of any society, according to Devlin, are the judgments any right-minded person will make on moral matters. The right-minded person, in turn, will be the ordinary man in the street, or, in Devlin's phrase, "the man in the Clapham bus."[4] Devlin maintains that we use the jury system to determine guilt, the jury being an institutional arrangement to realize the judgment of society. A similar device, hypothetical in form, can be used to say what is moral and what is not. Since morals are, by Devlin's definition, the fundamental units of consensus in society, any hypothetical group of ordinary people will be able to pronounce authentic judgments on moral matters. Like social contract theories, no specific congregation of ordinary people need form to pass judgment. The test, stated hypothetically, is sufficient to establish what morality means for Devlin. It is what the members of any society maintain *in fact* is moral. Further, the warranting measure for stamping out vice, in Devlin's argument, is the feeling of disgust which the man on the Clapham bus feels for certain practices he regards as immoral.

2. AGAINST THE ENFORCEMENT OF MORALS

Before criticizing Devlin's argument, it is important to stress what kind of an argument it is. It is logically possible to argue that morality, because it is morality, ought to be enforced by the law regardless of its effect on society's survival. This version of the enforcement argument rests on the

[4]Devlin, *The Enforcement of Morals*, p. 15.

intrinsic good of morality, rating it beyond the good of anything else. It is an extreme claim, palatable only to those who would rather be morally good than anything else, even survive. Devlin does not make this argument.[5] His argument is a more moderate one, though not (as we shall see) without its own extreme moments. Devlin argues that the enforcement of morals is warranted because morality plays such a vital role in the survival of a society, and any society is warranted in preserving itself. Thus it is not morality as such which justifies the enforcement of morals, but the empirical connection of morality to society added to a premise on self-preservation.

The obvious place to begin a critical exploration of Devlin's argument is with the two statements which comprise the premises for the conclusion on enforcement. They are (a) that a fundamental agreement on moral matters is necessary for the survival of a society, and (b) that a society is justified in preserving itself. The first statement is an empirical claim which most available evidence fails to support. If some fundamental agreement, or consensus, on anything were necessary to the survival of a society, a number of flourishing, or at least existing, societies would have gone under some time ago. Empirical surveys have shown time and again that consensus is an elusive, even quixotic, foundation for a society on any issue. Morality is not immune from this dissensus. Moral codes obviously vary not only in what "officially" counts as moral, but also on what people do in spite of conventional morality. Logically it is certainly possible for people to join in social arrangements simply for the sake of convenience in doing so, even survival, without agreeing on all, or any, moral issues. Think for a moment of how most people, at one age or another, get along with their parents: by ignoring certain moral issues. This "going along to get along" is certainly a possible pattern a society might take, where moral issues are submerged to the goal of harmony. None of this is meant to suggest that societies are never moral, or that moral issues may not on occasion precipitate severe social conflicts. All these remarks do is suggest possible social arrangements, supportable with empirical evidence, which then as possible arrangements deny the *necessary* connection Devlin asserts for moral consensus and survival.[6]

What Devlin seems to do is conflate two very different issues: (a) the

---

[5]This is recognized by H. L. A. Hart in what is the best critique of Devlin, *Law, Liberty, and Morality* (New York: Random House, Inc., 1963), pp. 5–6. I have relied on Hart's criticism at several points in my own critique of Devlin, footnoting Hart whenever this occurs, though in passages with no footnotes I am, so far as I know, developing my own line of thought.

[6]Hart severs Devlin's necessary connection between law and morality with the concept of "paternalism." I have used "convenience," though any concept will do which explains or justifies law without resort to morality.

morality of an action, and (b) the consequences of an action for the survival of a society. Some actions which are moral are undoubtedly of vital concern for a society's survival. Unrestricted killing is both a moral and a survival issue. But notice that even when an issue presents both moral and survival considerations it is still possible to view the issue in terms of one set of considerations or another. Prohibitions against murder can be justified solely in terms of survival considerations, or solely in terms of moral considerations. Either justification will make sense on its own without reliance on the other. When an action does not present both moral and survival issues the separation between the two kinds of justification is even more pronounced. Some practices may be immoral yet have no recognizable bearing on survival, as homosexual practices, for example. Now it is true that Devlin wants to see all immoral practices as "weakening." But this too is an empirical claim difficult to sustain. The only debilitating effect of homosexual practices may be the punitive actions taken by society against homosexuals, and this can hardly be taken then as evidence for the debilitating effects of homosexuality leading to a justification of punitive measures by society. Also, in complex societies homosexual practices in certain professions may be the conventional norm, not deviant at all and perhaps even moral on local standards while immoral on the general standards of the society. In such cases we have immoral practices which may not be harmful to the individual or a threat to society's survival. Turning full circle the other way we can identify practices which threaten a society's survival but are not immoral. If a society morally accepts birth control practices, and is in danger of not surviving because birth rates do not equal death rates (something hard to imagine today but not uncommon in the past), then a moral practice, or at least a practice which is not morally condemned, may constitute a survival threat. It is impossible to avoid the conclusion that there are two distinct issues in Devlin's argument, one moral, the other survival.

How is it that Devlin has fused the two so erroneously into one? The answer is that his conception of society does not allow for morally dysfunctional actions, or for moral actions with no public consequences.[7] Every moral action, for Devlin, has a positive bearing on the survival considerations of society exactly as it is moral, and a negative bearing exactly as it is immoral. In effect this view makes survival requisites and a society's moral system logical equivalents. Not only, however, are they two separate systems, as shown by the possibilities that (a) moral action can be dysfunctional, and (b) immoral action can be unrelated to survival, and perhaps even functional, but we can also easily imagine a society

[7]Hart distinguishes between the immorality of an act and its status as a public nuisance. Hart, *Law, Liberty, and Morality,* pp. 43–48.

destroying part of its moral system in order to survive. An authoritarian society, for example, may well legalize and encourage abortion to cope with a population problem even in the face of moral convictions contrary to abortion. The prospects of such a policy's success may be given low marks without denying the possibility of a conflict between the moral system and the society's survival requisites. The possibility of such a conflict can be denied only by defining a society in terms of its moral convictions.[8]   How such a definition can be supported is difficult to imagine, however, since in any society of any modest complexity changes may occur in the society which do not require changes in the moral code, as for example shifts from rural to urban living patterns. This being so, a part of society is not normally reducible to its moral code, thus allowing for a possible conflict between some dimensions of a society and that dimension defined by the moral code.

One problem in this first premise of Devlin's argument is in the idea of "survival." It is reasonable to allow that a breach in morality will constitute, and possibly result in, certain changes in a society (though the possibility that some immoral actions have no appreciable effect on a society cannot be disallowed either). These changes may even be harmful on the criteria of worthiness set out in the moral system. But it is a second order of seriousness to elevate these changes to threats on the very survival of a society. What is it for a society to fail to survive? We can imagine natural disasters which wipe away whole populations, and the like, but this is not the failure which Devlin has in mind. Suppose a society's moral code alters completely, bringing with it a change in the general way of life characterizing that society. Has the society failed to survive? Something has certainly failed to survive, though other things obviously have. People go on living, even if things are not the same as they were. If this is what is meant by the failure to survive, however, then defending a society's right to "survive" becomes very difficult. Since morality is, for Devlin, the moral convictions of any conventional arrangements, then these arrangements can only be justified in terms of the ongoing moral system. But a new moral system will then have its own justification, and we have no means for saying that one moral system, and the "way of life" of which it is a part, is any better than any other. Far from a defense of a society's right to preserve itself, Devlin's account of morality gives us no defense for one moral system as opposed to another, nor one "way of life" as opposed to another.

This point against Devlin is made by allowing immoral activity to threaten a society's "survival." It is more reasonable to imagine something less serious, that moral change or immoral behavior will on occa-

---

[8]Hart, ·Law, Liberty, and Morality, pp. 48–52.

sion affect only some parts of a society and not its "way of life." The following classification may be helpful. Some moral actions are vital to institutions in themselves, as promise-keeping is to contracts. Other moral actions are vital in terms of general performance norms, as sobriety. Actions vital in themselves help define an institution, as part of what we mean by a contract is keeping a promise, and any breach of the moral code definitionally within an institution will automatically threaten the institution. General performance principles, on the other hand, can be violated without necessarily damaging any institution. A society can tolerate successfully a number of drunks, or even some drinking among all its members. Only when substantial numbers of people are drunks will a society begin to suffer. A third kind of moral action will have no public consequences. Disallowing Devlin's dubious claim for a necessary connection between weakness and immorality, sexual practices seem to have little if any empirical connections with the vitality of institutions or societies. Notice that even where morality is a vital part of an institution, as in promise-keeping and contracts, no comprehensive connection has been identified between a moral code and the vitality of a society. The kind of threat to survival Devlin envisages is as difficult to specify conceptually as it is to identify empirically.

The second of Devlin's premises presents still more difficulties. *Is* a society justified in preserving itself? One difficulty in answering this question, as we have seen, is settling on what preservation means. But we have seen that, whatever we mean by survival, or whatever we mean to preserve, the justification for this preservation will not be gotten out of a morality defined in conventional terms. To say that morals are the convictions fundamental to a society is to close out the possibility of justifying those convictions morally. What is required for the justification is a morality with the "external" feature identified in the last chapter. A morality with externality, not wholly defined by the factual convictions of any given society, will then be able to judge the society's "way of life" as worth preserving or not. But of course to open this inquiry is no guarantee of an affirmative response to any particular society. Whether a society should preserve itself will turn on what kind of a society it is, what kind of means are necessary for preservation, and what kind of substantive principles inform the external morality. It follows that Devlin's second premise, that a society is justified in preserving itself, is by no means the certain proposition he requires to reach his conclusion on the enforcement of morals.[9]

Devlin's account of morality is deficient also in other ways, part of this due to its simplicity. Moral convictions can be on (a) what counts as

---

[9]Hart, *Law, Liberty, and Morality,* pp. 17–20.

a moral issue, as for example whether abortion is to be covered by morality at all, and (b) the position taken on moral issues, as whether one is for or against abortions once the topic is admitted to moral discourse. Two quite different kinds of principles are involved in each type of conviction above, principles which specify the scope of morality in (a) and principles which justify action in (b). When this dichotomy is added to the earlier mentioned distinctions between consensus on principles and consensus on actions consistent with principles (as agreement on the abstract principle of freedom is not yet agreement on which actions are free), distinctions between moral approbation of acts done privately *vs.* done publicly (as one may condone homosexual behavior, but not on St. Mark's Square), the different points of consensus locatable along an intensity scale (as two people may both be against gambling, but in disagreement over how serious the vice is), the disagreement possible over means (how to implement moral values), and many other sources of disagreement, it can be seen that the model of consensus constructed by Devlin will not be an adequate account of morals in even the simplest societies and the thought of some moral code homogeneous on all these dimensions approaches the limits of credibility.

It is also not clear why "disgust" must be included in morality at all. Devlin suggests that the test for whether an immoral practice should be regulated is the feeling of "disgust" by the man in the Clapham bus. But surely we can all be disgusted at things unrelated to morality. Someone who purposely eats rotten food for no good reason is disgusting by common standards. He is not, however, immoral. On the other hand, many immoral practices are not disgusting, in the sense of eliciting nausea, or deeply offending the sensibilities. Cheating on one's mate is ordinarily considered immoral, but the emotions it typically arouses are closer to anger, pity, frustration, than to disgust. It might be a useful thing if every immoral practice was disgusting. But it would also be dangerous to tag immorality with such a feeling. Suppose the man on the Clapham bus is *not* disgusted by aerial bombings of cities in war? Does this then allow the action to escape the net of morality? Fortunately we have other defining signs for immoral action than the rare and exaggerated posture of disgust on which Devlin relies.

It is the inadequate conceptualization of morality which provides for the surface plausibility of Devlin's case. If something is immoral then of course it ought not to be done; and if it ought not to be done we can marshall any of a number of reasons (including, perhaps, survival) for outlawing it. But if our picture of morality were an accurate one, we would see quickly that the law is ill equipped to enforce morals. One can enforce a moral code, insuring that people behave in accordance with the values of the code. But, as has already been pointed out in the last chapter, a person can *be* moral only by freely acting in a moral way. So what might be the most valuable component in a moral system, the state of mind which goes along with moral agency, is effectively excluded with the external enforcement carried out by law. If morality were properly seen as a prescriptive system, requiring as prescriptions supporting reasons to convince and not coerce agents, then enforcement would immediately be seen as an inappropriate device to realize moral action.

2.1. The case against Devlin can be summed up as follows. (1) A fundamental agreement on moral matters does not seem necessary for the definition of a society. (2) Moral and survival considerations are different species of reasons in different systems of reasoning. (3) A society is not automatically justified in preserving itself, and can be warranted in doing so only with an "external" morality not covered by Devlin's definition of morality. (4) Legal enforcement deprives moral action of its "inner" quality of moral agency. Fundamental to the difficulties identified in Devlin's argument is his faulty conceptualization of morality. Two of the four features of morality set out in the last chapter, "externality" and "prescriptiveness," reveal some of the major problems in Devlin's case for enforcement.

3. NONMORAL POLITICS

These points against Devlin should not obscure the close factual relationship between law and morality. It is an indisputable matter that morality has influenced law historically and comprises a common justification for legal norms. But to concede this is not to concede anything on the question of whether law ought to be used to enforce morals. The issue of enforcement is a *conceptual* issue, its dimensions determined by the definitional status of morality in the concept of society and how morality itself is conceptualized. Looking closely at these concepts presents little advantage to the enforcement partisans, the arguments appearing to be decisively against enforcement. The problems for the enforcement supporters seem to occur even before the arguments begin, for to talk of law enforcing morals is already to accept the separation between two societal systems (law and morality) which later does so much damage to the survival claims of the enforcement position.

It can be illuminating to ask a different question entirely. Instead of "Ought law to enforce morals?," one might ask, "What is the form of a moral law?" This second question is distinct from the enforcement question in not presupposing the damaging distinction between legal and moral systems. Rather it poses the question of what a law looks like which realizes the requirements of morality, thus fusing the two systems. This second question, however, is to be carefully distinguished from the question of whether a law must assume the defining features of morality in order to be a law. This latter "definitional" question was discussed earlier, in Chapter Three, in the claim by Lon Fuller that law, to be law, must embody moral properties. It was argued then, and can be reaffirmed now, that legal systems can be adequately explained with nonmoral considerations and that a definitional fusion of law and morality obscures some of the more important features of law (its possible conflict with morality, for example). But, affirming this, it still may be asked what law which *is* moral looks like. What is the form of that special kind of law, not exhaustive of law generally, which does embody the features of morality?

At this point it is instructive to broaden the discussion somewhat. Instead of concentrating simply on law, this question on form can be directed at society itself. There are two advantages to this. First, an important criticism of Devlin was occasioned by the separation between the larger society and its moral system (which then made logically possible a conflict between the survival of the society and the maintenance of its moral system). The prospect of a hypothetical fusion between law and morality will avoid the particular difficulty in Devlin's argument of law conflicting with morality, but the possibility of the social and fused legal-moral systems conflicting remains present. If the question is broadened to ask, "What is the form of a moral society?," then this internal conflict is avoided. Second, to ask the larger question of what a moral society looks like is to move this inquiry closer to the tradition of normative political inquiry which the positivist thesis on values has discredited. It is generally acknowledged that the history of political theory prior to this century has been concerned to describe the just or moral polity. Contemporary political inquiry, on the assumption that value statements do not make truth claims, has largely excluded *that* kind of normative inquiry from the aegis of legitimacy. The discussion here has been concerned to demonstrate the limitations of positivism and the alternatives to it. It is a natural extension of the discussion to revive the traditional emphasis on the good polity with the analytic tools introduced so far, exploring not how one dimension of a society, the law, can be moral but how the larger society itself can be moral. Though nothing like the detail and rigor of the great political philosophers of the past should be expected in these brief pages, at least the question itself suggests a continuation of the normative tradition in political theory ignored in this century.

3.1. Let us, to be thorough, approach the question of a normative polity along the longer road of the nonmoral society. From the earlier (Chapter Four) discussion of morality it is reasonable to conclude that an action may be nonmoral on either of two grounds: (a) as irrelevant to morality, or (b) as an exception to a moral prescription. Most social events will probably fall into the category of irrelevance. Eating meals, sleeping, going to work, driving one's car, these and a multitude of other actions are irrelevant to moral concerns. One can imagine a society where no distinction is maintained between moral relevance and irrelevance. But, while logically possible, such a society would deny the important capacity of moral language to single out some actions as more important than others. To say of something that it is a moral issue is to invest it with a gravity, even at times an urgency, which other issues do not have. This important function of moral language can be exercised only as a sense of moral relevance is maintained, something the function reflects and which does seem typical in social discourse given the obvious distinctions between actions like aimlessly strolling down the street and killing pedestrians aimlessly.

Morally irrelevant actions may intersect with morality in a number of ways. Speeding in one's automobile may be a violation only of traffic regulations, which may in turn by explained and defended simply in terms of the prudential consideration of convenience. But if one has an accident while speeding which costs innocent bystanders their lives, then speeding has become a moral issue because of its consequences. Some morally irrelevant actions intersect with morality in terms of meta-considerations. For example, the prosecution of a man for delinquency in his alimony payments may be a morally irrelevant event where the woman does not need the money, but become a moral issue where due process is not observed in the courtroom. *What* the issue is can be considered morally irrelevant on its own though *how* it is handled, the meta-consideration of procedure, can be a moral issue. Also, some actions may be morally irrelevant in themselves but constitute resolutions to moral issues. A moral dispute which has public consequences may be legally regulated on the grounds of social harmony, which may itself be a nonmoral consideration. Notice, however, that in each of these intersection cases the morally irrelevant events are now morally relevant, perhaps even moral, though still viewable as nonmoral because of their status as morally irrelevent events when they do *not* intersect with morality. The consequences, meta-considerations, and regulative objects of the actions are moral. Only as we *do* accept the nonmorality of the events do the intersection cases make sense. And of course many morally irrelevant actions do not intersect even remotely with morality, as for example in driving one's car without incident.

The second kind of nonmoral action, exceptions, are unlike the first in being morally relevant types of action which are nonmoral by virtue of extenuating circumstances. Killing, for example, is normally prohibited on moral grounds. Yet it is also normally defeasible by a proof of self-defense. Self-defense can be considered an exception to the moral prohibition against killing. (Whether one is willing to accept self-defense as an actual exception is irrelevant here. What is important is the logic of exceptions, not what counts substantively as an exception.) An exception is an event normally covered by a moral prescription, relevant to morality in the sense of being a moral action on normal occasions, yet not governed by morality because of special circumstances which defeat the moral ought.

It is worth noticing again how the logic of moral discourse is not reducible to the true-false view of statements contained in positivism. A defeating proposition does not falsify a moral prescription, or even discredit it in any way. We are not suddenly left with a worthless rule enjoining killing just because self-defense sets the rule aside. The no-killing edict still holds in all circumstances where there is no exception. On a strict true-false view of statements, such a process of acceptance and deflection is impossible. Either no-killing is a true statement, and thus worth keeping, or it is false, and thus to be rejected. The "defeating" process accommodates another set of criteria for handling statements. A moral prescription binds action in all relevant cases where no statements can be adduced to justify an exception. Where an exception is demonstrated the event is nonmoral, though the moral prescription remains valid. We keep it, but we do not use it on the particular occasion of an exception.[10]

3.2. It may be thought that moral prescription tolerates no exceptions, that the moral thing to do is the thing to do regardless. But this view is impossible to maintain for two reasons. First, one can never tell, in the oldest of clichés, what the future will bring. A rule prescribing anything may at some point encounter an unanticipated event which on any of a number of grounds we may want to call an exception. The fitting of rules to experience can be seen in terms of continuing judgments as to what counts under the rule, what does not, and what is an exception to it. It is logically possible, and perhaps historically accurate, to see no-killing prohibitions as carved out of experience to govern experience; and then, as governors of experience, the edict must be withheld from experiences not covered by the rule (killing animals perhaps), held as relevant though an exception to some experiences covered by the rule (killing in self-defense, say), and made to bind in relevant cases where no defeating conditions occur (premeditated murder, say). The precise guidelines for making these distinctions surely emerge as the rule is used in experience. To say, without qualification, that moral prescriptions have no exceptions is in effect to assert that the above distinctions arising in the use of a rule can all be anticipated beforehand, something which is clearly untenable.

[10]The idea of "defeasibility" I have taken from Hart, "The Ascription of Responsibilities and Rights," in *Logic and Language* (Oxford: Basil Blackwell, 1960), ed. by Anthony Flew, pp. 145–66.

Second, the principles by which exceptions occur can be stated as part of the logic of rules. The most extreme ground for an exception is the possibility that rules will encounter paradoxical situations. In the most famous example of this, one used as seminal idea in a whole philosophical movement, a spectator fortuitously armed sees another armed man about to kill a third. Assuming the innocence of the potential victim, and assuming that the only way the killing of the third man can be halted is by the spectator transforming himself into agent and killing the would-be murderer, then the spectator is in a situation whose outcome is unavoidably the violation of a no-killing edict. If he does nothing, the victim is killed. If he acts to save the victim, he must kill the victimizer. In either case the rule against killing is broken. Students of existentialism will recognize this type of example, where extreme choices must be made through action with no effective rule for guidance, as the paradigmatic event for that philosophy. The issue here is not whether such events are paradigmatic or atypical extremes. It is simply that the possibility of such a paradox will then make exceptions possible; for where it is impossible to follow a no-killing rule and the action is still relevant to the rule (as sharpening pencils is not relevant to a no-killing rule), then it is reasonable to view the paradox as an exception to the moral rule.

Paradoxes are not the happiest origins for philosophical claims. The requirement of exceptions in moral discourse can be defended in more prosaic terms. Rules, or (in this case) prescriptions, are supportable with reasons. The reason for a prescription may always logically function as the reason for an exception to the prescription.[11] For example, the prescription, "everyone ought to pay their taxes" can be supported with the reason "Because the revenues are used to benefit those in need." Now if this is accepted as a reason for paying taxes, then when the reason does not obtain, when, in this case, revenues are not used to benefit those in need, then one is not obligated to pay taxes. As with the self-defense example, the validity of the reason is not at issue. The reader should feel free to substitute any reason he wishes to test the logic. The point is that stating a reason for an *ought* is to state the empirical conditions in which the *ought* binds. When these conditions do not obtain, then we have an exception to the prescription. The exception will be conditions relevant to the prescription in the sense of being normally covered by the *ought,* but the obligation on the agent is defeated because the reason for the *ought* is not realized in the conditions. Some reasons will entertain exceptions only in the remotest sense of being logically possible. If I accept that taxes ought to be paid because governments require money to operate, then I have supported the prescription with a reason so general as to defy defeat. But reasons must be empirical statements, not tautologies.

[11]Marcus Singer, *Generalization in Ethics, op. cit.,* p. 124.

(Otherwise we do not have a reason for action but a definition of the prescription's subject, *viz.,* governments are agencies which by definition need money.) Empirical statements may always be otherwise, for, as explained in Chapter One, the contrary of an empirical statement is never a contradiction. Thus *any* reason, by virtue of the fact that it is an empirical statement, will provide for an exception through the possibility that its contrary may come to be the case, however remote the possibility in an actual case. It is always possible, in our example, even though unlikely, that governments may not require money to operate; and if one has accepted that as a reason for paying taxes, then if that contrary possibility occurs the reason vanishes and so does the obligation to pay taxes.

3.3. It may also be thought that exceptions are really alternative moral prescriptions. Self-defense, for example, may be thought to be bound by yet another moral principle prescribing what ought to be done in conditions describable as self-defense. But this thought is uninformed. An exception to a moral rule is not bound by a moral principle. It is a situation which escapes from moral direction because of its special features. Consider what it is to be morally guided. If one's actions are prescribed by a moral principle, then the particular features of the situation in which one acts are not overriding. The moral ought is overriding, requiring that the situation is viewed as relevantly similar to all other situations governed by the universal ought. To be guided, for example, by the no-killing principle means (a) one does not kill because one is following the moral ought against killing (the principle overrides the particular features of the situation), and (b) the conditions in which one acts are part of the descriptive class of situations bound by the no-killing prohibitions (relevant similarity obtains).

Now consider what it is to act in terms of an exception to a moral prescription. The first characteristic of an exception is that it is parasitic on a moral principle. Self-defense makes no sense as an exception unless it is seen in terms of an enjoinment against killing which has been defeated. In the general sense of the term, all exceptions presume the prior acceptance of rules. An exception in moral discourse presumes the prior acceptance of a moral prescription in the absence of which the exception has no meaning. Second, an exception is an action guided not by principle, but by the particular features of the conditions in which action occurs. If something is an exception to a moral prescription it is because its particular features are warranted in defeating the moral ought, setting the ought aside on *this* occasion here and now (though still with binding force on other occasions where defeating conditions are not present). Exceptions may be guided by rules, as self-defense is typically bound by strict legal rules setting out the range of permissible actions. Other kinds of exceptions are less bound, perhaps even rule-less, as exceptions to any rule for raising children may be so various in what is permitted as to call for spontaneous action. But the rules for exceptions, no matter how strict or how loose, are still rules for acting in particular situations, where the particulars of the situation are the decisive considerations. To act on principle is to override these particular considerations. Third, exceptions are relevantly dissimilar to those situations where the moral principle at issue binds. If self-defense were like those situations covered by a no-killing principle in all the relevant respects, then it would not be an exception to the principle. It is possible that exceptions may be like one another, coverable by descriptive criteria which classify types of exceptions. Any particular act of self-defense, for example, may be relevantly similar to all other actions falling under the term "self-defense." Or, on the other hand, some exceptions may be in a class by themselves, *sui generis,* as certain charismatic leaders seem to be on occasion. But in all cases an exception must be relevantly dissimilar to the class of cases where moral guidance occurs.

It follows from these features of an exception that exceptions cannot be disguised moral principles. First, exceptions are subsequent to moral principles and parasitic on them, not principles in their own right. Second, and as a consequence of the parasitic quality, both moral principles and exceptions may be held simultaneously even though they represent contrary courses of action (no-killing *vs.* killing). It is impossible to hold two contrary moral principles simultaneously since an acceptance of one will by definition mean a rejection of the other. An exception does not require the rejection of a moral principle. It requires, on the contrary, its maintenance, since an exception exists in terms of the moral principle. An exception is a defeating circumstance, consistent with the acceptance of the defeated moral principle, a consistency impossible with a contrary moral principle. Third, an exception represents the preeminence of particular conditions over principle, while a moral principle must override the particulars of a situation to guide action. Fourth, an exception contains no *ought,* which is what a moral principle is by definition. One is not bound to defend oneself under pain of being immoral, which is what would be required were self-defense a moral principle. One is merely bound by certain rules of action *if* one chooses to defend oneself. Fifth, exceptions may or may not be rule-guided and describable with criteria of sameness, while moral action must be rule-guided and describable in terms of sameness criteria. For all of these reasons an exception is not a disguised moral principle, but rather represents a distinctive kind of action and considerations for reasoning.

4. INCREMENTALISM AS A NONMORAL POLICY

If policy is to be nonmoral it must assume one of the two forms identified here: either it must be (a) irrelevant to morality, or (b) an exception to a moral prescription. It is reasonable to suppose that most policies are nonmoral in the first sense, as ordinarily having little, if anything, to do with morality. Even the briefest reflections on law, and social policy generally, will reveal that morality is irrelevant to most of the rules and directives of social action. Traffic regulations, zoning ordinances, business licenses, these and so many other things ordinarily have no relevance to moral issues. On the other hand, political issues like franchise extension, minimum wages, tax schedules, are often argued in terms of moral principles. Those social policies which are relevant to morality can be nonmoral only in terms of the second sense of nonmorality listed above, the logical form of an exception.

One of the common distinctions in policy analysis is between the "classical" and incrementalist models of policy. A classical policy model is one in which (a) the ends of policy are hierarchically ordered, (b) the means to realize these ends are ranked, (c) perfect information is assumed, and (d) rationality is the carrying out of ends through this system of ranked means and perfect information. The classical model may be a device either to govern preferences or to express and realize preferences. Plato, for example, assumed that ends are discovered in a natural hierarchy, these ends then to govern demands. Other classicists, on the other hand, may see ends as chosen and arranged hierarchically, the model then functioning as an arrangement for making decisions.[12] All versions of the classical model share these two ideas, however: first, that ends and means can be ordered on the basis of perfect information, and, second, that action can be directed by an imperative deduced from this arrangement of means and ends.

The incrementalist tradition has opposed the classical model of policy largely on the grounds that it is not a feasible way of making and implementing decisions. Karl Popper, for example, advances a proof against historicism (which Popper takes as the embodiment of the classical model) summarized in the following equation: $Y = f(X, Z)$, where Y is the future, X is human knowledge, and Z all other influences.[13] It is impossible, Popper maintains, ever to predict the future with anything

---

[12]Charles Lindblom, in *The Policy-Making Process* (Englewood Cliffs, N.J.: Prentice-Hall, Inc., 1968), p. 13, outlines one preference version of the classical model. A more elaborate statement on some classical models of policy can be found in the first three chapters of David Braybrooke and Charles Lindblom, *A Strategy of Decision* (New York: The Free Press, 1963).

[13]Karl Popper, *The Poverty of Historicism* (London: Routledge, Kegan Paul, 1959). The equation is a summary of Popper's claim in the preface, pp. v–vii.

like perfect success because of the unpredictability of X, human knowledge. If, as the equation states, the future is a function of the growth of human knowledge and all other influences, then even if all other influences can be predicted, the future still cannot be on the basis of the unpredictability of human knowledge. For Popper, then, the classical model is not feasible because of the impossibility of ever attaining perfect information, even in principle. The result, in Popper's philosophy, is a model of policy labeled "piecemeal engineering," in which social change is marginal and short-range, the only model for Popper which is justifiable with imperfect knowledge.

Later developments in the incrementalist tradition accept that social experience is unpredictable and then add on to this thesis additional limitations for policy. Herbert Simon, for example, describes the limitations of any agent who makes policy, such as limitations of performance and intellect. Simon also stresses environmental limitations, the unavoidable costs of action, and the changed considerations which result whenever action is initiated. The model of policy which, for Simon, accommodates these limitations is a "sufficing" one, where action is "good enough" for the particular conditions in which it occurs but not perfect by any absolute standards.[14]   David Braybrooke and Charles Lindblom extend these constraints on action into a model of policy based on marginal choice, a restriction in considered alternatives (both in variety and number), continual adjustment of objectives, reconstruction of data, and serial, remedial, and socially fragmented analysis. Here the term "incrementalism" is used explicitly.[15]

Though, as with any tradition, there is much to distinguish among these alternatives to the classical model, they all have in common several features. These are (a) a denial of the possibility of perfect knowledge, (b) the rejection, as a consequence of this denial, of imperatives for action deduced from hierarchically arranged values, and (c) the assumption that the conditions in which policy is implemented override *a priori* rules or principles. It is precisely this preeminence of social conditions, as opposed to social rules or principles, which permits only "piecemeal engineering" (Popper), "sufficing" action (Simon), or "incremental" planning (Braybrooke-Lindblom) instead of the classical way of making and implementing policy.

As the brief descriptions above suggest, the case for incrementalism against the classical model is based largely on feasibility considerations. (It is not so much that the classical model is moral or immoral, but that

---

[14]Herbert Simon, *Administrative Behavior* (New York: The Macmillan Company, 1959).
[15]Braybrooke and Lindblom, *A Strategy of Decision.*

it is, according to the incrementalists, impossible.) It is easy to see, however, how the alternatives to the classical approach are nonmoral in their logical form. One of the defining features of an exception to a moral prescription, as we have seen, is that the conditions in which action occurs override the moral principle. This overridingness of realizing conditions, the preeminence of social experience, is also one of the defining features of incremental policy. Now it may be thought that some slight-of-hand is about to occur, in that two things may still have a common feature without one being identified as a version of the other, as both chess and baseball are played with players, though nothing important about one is true of the other because of this. But the common feature shared by incrementalism and an exception to a moral presecription is decisive in setting aside moral direction. If the particular conditions of action are allowed to override any *a priori* directives or guides for action, then moral action is impossible on the account of morality elaborated and defended here. When the issue occasioning action is a moral issue, then *not* acting on moral principle must then be either immoral or nonmoral. The elevation, in incrementalism, of social conditions to a preeminent level is to require that incrementalist policy be of a form that is not moral. It can be (a) irrelevant to morality (where social issues are not moral issues) or (b) nonmoral (where warranting criteria allow particular conditions to defeat a relevant moral prescription). What incrementalism cannot be is a moral form of policy. The importance of this observation is that, if the incremental model is applied to moral issues and an exception *is* justified, then incrementalism will be the logical form of nonmoral policy making and execution, a form which has been given the title "reason of state" in the history of political theory.

In opposition to these observations it might be said by supporters of incrementalism that incremental policy is the best way of realizing both *a priori* rules or principles and ends. A holistic policy, by virtue of its inherent lack of feasibility, is likely to fare worse on rational grounds in implementing any value. Thus a polity practicing incremental policy is one most likely to bring about moral solutions, precisely because it is more rational than the classical method of policy enactment, and on these grounds it can be viewed as more moral than alternative policy forms. It is important to keep in mind, however, that supporters of incrementalism, no matter what else they maintain, must hold to proposition (c) above: that the conditions in which policy is implemented are more important considerations than *a priori* rules, principles, *or* goals. One of the main points scored against the classicists by incrementalists is that they (the classicists) do not recognize the importance of what occurs as policy is implemented. For Braybrooke and Lindblom the policy process suggests not only realistic constraints on implementation, but also new goals.

An especially troublesome feature of the synoptic ideal was its failure to adapt to the frequency with which problems arise not in situations where goal achievement is frustrated and alternative new routes are sought . . . but instead in situations in which some new policy possibility is put forward. . . . What is required is not new policies to reach a goal *but new goals toward which to employ a policy.*[16] (Italics added.)

If action (in the form of implementation) is the source of rules, principles, or goals, however, then principles do not govern action. They are the servants of action. In such a case the principled type of prescription found in morality has been denied. It is remarkable how similar the incrementalist case is to the logical form of an exception to moral prescription, which warrants the preeminence of particular conditions, the concrete here-and-now stressed by incrementalists. In both cases principles are subordinated to the considerations (moral and feasibility) encountered in an implementation process.

It is helpful to keep distinct the following three questions. First, ought law (or social policy) to be used to enforce morality? Second, which techniques of policy implementation will best bring about moral ends? Third, what is the form of moral social arrangements? The first question was discussed earlier in this chapter. The second is a complicated issue which will not be discussed here. It can be conceded that the feasibility case argued by incrementalist theorists can be used to support incrementalism as the best (most rational) means to achieve moral ends, perhaps as a "start-and-stop" process realistically winding its way toward a moral goal. But of course this is a different question from the third question above, is incrementalism itself a form of moral social arrangements? I have argued that it cannot be in raising the strategy of adaptation to a higher level than governing principles (principles which can logically be contrary to feasibility considerations). My argument, however, is still compatible with incrementalism as a nonmoral, and perhaps eminently rational, means to realize moral ends.

5. THE MORAL POLITY

If incrementalism is the logical form of nonmoral politics, then what is the form of moral politics? Notice that this, the third question posed above, is the question Plato asked. The *Republic* is not a device to enforce justice (question one above), or a means to acquire justice (question two above). It *is* justice, defined in terms of social arrangements. What follows, however, will be Platonic only in its attempt to outline an answer to the same question Plato asked, nothing more. No theory of forms will be presumed, and nothing like Plato's comprehensiveness and

---

[16]Braybrooke and Lindblom, *A Strategy of Decision,* p. 142.

rigor will even be attempted. The exercise below is nothing more than an extension to aggregate dimensions of the defining features of morality stated earlier, or the use of these features as descriptions of a society. The result should be a sketch of the moral polity.

(a) The first feature of a moral polity must be public consistency and similarity on the criteria of the principles used to direct or guide action in policy. It is easy to misunderstand this descriptive requirement. Actions do not have to be identical to be covered by the same moral prescription. Some principles will require a uniformity of performance, as in promise-keeping, while others will permit a substantial diversity in performance, as "Love your neighbor." But the actions covered by a principle must be consistent with one another in not permitting contrary action, as both smashing your neighbor and kissing your neighbor are not ordinarily consistent actions. Also, the conditions in which actions occur must be relevantly alike in not containing defeating factors. A polity consisting of exceptions to moral prescriptions is not, by definition, a polity which realizes moral principles. Again, this requirement does not mean that all events are consistent and similar. Only those events directed or guided by moral *oughts, public* events as moral *oughts* are policy *oughts,* are covered by this requirement. Private events, and even social experience which is public on other criteria and not a matter of public policy, are not bound by consistency or similarity.

(b) Second, the highest source of morality in a moral polity is located in public events. If public policy can be seen as the prescriptive system for society generally, then moral policy will override all contrary actions in the area in which it is implemented. This description is not a denial of private morality. It is a statement of supremacy. Whenever public and private moral claims conflict, it is necessary in a moral polity that the public claim prevail if policy is to be a set of overriding rules for society. It follows that a moral polity can permit moral freedom only in areas not covered by policy. It is important to see that the degree of moral freedom permitted in a moral polity is a consequence of the *scope* of policy, not the fact that the policy is moral. So private morality, and moral freedom, are logically possible in a moral polity, though not in matters affecting policy. Public events are the highest sources of morality in the sense that the morals contained in policy prevail whenever public and private issues collide. This denial of moral freedom on policy issues is required by making moral principles an official fact. When moral principles are matters of public policy, then moral evaluation in the area of policy is like factual evaluation: a matter of convention. It was pointed out earlier (Chapter One) that the absence of an entailment between facts and evaluations provides for the possibility of moral freedom. In a moral polity dissent from the conventional judgments of policy on moral grounds is impossible, for the facts of policy *are* the principles of morality. Thus, as stated above, moral freedom is possible in a moral polity only in terms of (in Hobbes' phrase) "the silence of the law," at least on issues with implications for policy.

(c) A moral polity will be universal in scope. If moral universals are to be taken as applying to all men as such, and not to men in their particular roles or characteristics, then the policy propositions and structural arrangements comprising a moral polity are right for all men. No *normative* distinction can be made between citizens (those men legally subject to policy) and noncitizens (those men not legally subject to policy). A factual distinction may exist in that a society which is moral will find it impossible to modify anyone's behavior except those within the zone of its effective power, a zone that may have clear limits short of all mankind. So a moral polity may still be an empirical unit in being distinguishable from other social arrangements. Nevertheless, the logic of morality requires that action done on a moral principle must be right for all. So a moral polity must rest on the conviction that its arrangements for action are universally prescriptive, unless shown otherwise with a demonstration of relevant dissimilarity.

(d) The moral polity will also be nonheroic. The extraordinary man or action, in the public sphere, violates the public similarity which moral policy requires. Iris Murdock has said: "If one is Napoleon one does not think that everyone should do as one does oneself."[17] Napoleons can be treated with purely rational prescriptions, and with defeats for moral prescriptions. The rule of sameness, "Treat like cases alike" has been observed when unlike cases are treated in unlike fashion. So to say that Napoleons deserve special treatment is a rational judgment. It is also a judgment which, as an exception, may fall under other sameness criteria, as in the reasonable requirement that *if* there are other Napoleons they must be treated in the same way. Napoleon judgments will also fit moral reasoning, though only as exceptions. A prescription for all men is defeated by a Napoleon if by a Napoleon we mean a man relevantly dissimi-

---

[17]Murdoch, "Vision and Choice in Morality," *Dreams and Self-Knowledge,* Aristotelian Society, Supplementary Vol. 30 (1956), pp. 32–58. It can also be pointed out here that a universalizable model of morality *does* come closest to the requirements of policy. It has been pointed out by Alasdair MacIntyre that private morality and supererogatory actions are excluded from the universalizability model. This is precisely what I am at pains to show here, that to universalize is to legislate on the basis of relevant similarity—an obvious parallel with policy. What I am trying to demonstrate is that a version of morality so clearly similar to policy nevertheless results in special kinds of political arrangements not exhaustive of politics generally. Further, private and supererogatory actions, while possible inclusions in policy, still are unlike policy as a directive or guide for all. So to see these actions as exceptions is to see them in terms of their most important characteristics. See A. C. MacIntyre, "What Morality Is Not," *Philosophy* (October 1957), Vol. XXXII, pp. 325–35.

lar from all other men. So moral policy, as the effective implementation of moral principles, cannot countenance Napoleons in that it cannot countenance exceptions; for moral principles have not been implemented in exceptions. This point can be extended to supererogatory actions, which are moral though not binding on all men. A moral polity is a social arrangement of moral principles which *do* bind on all men generally, and bind in fact on the members of the moral polity. If saintliness is extraordinary, as it is, then it cannot be the basis for moral policy. Subnormal performance also is excluded from moral policy. In short, nothing extraordinary is contained in policy or the area directed by policy in a moral polity.

(e) A moral polity will also emphasize the general qualities of social experience at the expense of its particular features. Consider the general judgment, "All married couples who are still in school ought not to have children." Now make it less general, as "Joe and Sue, who are married and both students, ought not to have children." Now make it even more particular, as "Joe and Sue ought not to have had *this* child, Mary, the child which was born while they were students." It can be conceded that the issue is prejudiced by introducing an accomplished fact, the birth of a child, in the third *ought* judgment. But the general point can still be made without loss of effect. It is simply that a moral policy, as the effective implementation of moral prescriptions, will be the realization in action of principles or rules which override particular considerations. If *this* child in *this* situation escapes from under the prescription, and the escape is warranted, then an exception has occurred; and an exception is the defeat of a moral prescription, not its effective implementation. Thus a moral polity will, by definition, be characterized by the predominence of general rules and principles and the consequent subordination of particular considerations. It is not too difficult to see that a moral polity, as a result of this predominence, will consist of disinterested politics. It is not the point of view of any participant in action which is sustained in moral policy, but rather the rule or principle which comes *to* action as a prescription for what to do.

(f) Finally, the moral polity will subordinate demand to the principles of moral action. A moral proposition is a prescriptive statement, as we have seen, and thus never a simple demand. At the very least a moral proposition must have "enlightened," or some other suitable qualifier, in front of demand. The reason for this is that moral predicates never merely express wants or desires. They also govern them. (See Chapter Four.) So a demand can never in itself be the source of a moral directive. The criteria of governing, those principles which warrant prescriptivism, must also be a source of moral *oughts*. A nonmoral policy can originate entirely in simple demands, as action irrelevant to morality may be merely the direct satisfaction of wants. But a moral policy will fall outside a direct connection between simple demands and their satisfaction.

This descriptive feature can be seen more easily if politics is viewed for the moment through the language of systems theory. It is normally thought in systems theory that policy is circular as to origin and application.[18] By this is meant that the reciprocal connection between the authorities and the public is continuous. Policy is seen as a set of outputs directed at the public. These outputs then are connected to feedbacks from the public which are transformed into supports and demands. Supports and demands, in turn, are transformed into policy, though there can be an excess of demands (not all of them transformed into policy). However, it is less clear that there can be an excess of policy over demands. The reason for this is that policy in systems theory is conceptualized as a response to demands, either outside of (inputs) or within (withinputs) the space provided for authorities on the continuum. Now if this input-output model is taken to represent the satisfaction of simple demands, then it is an account of nonmoral politics. A moral polity will allow for a point of origin outside the connecting path between demands and policies. A moral principle may operate as an ideal demanded by no one in the society. It is an ideal which must be held by someone at the point of execution. But it need not be a demand prior to a policy output. The origins of policy may in this ideal sense be totally enclosed in that space on the continuum marking off merely the making of policy, and thus unconnected to demands. Even without the extremes of idealism, however, moral policy must always provide for some criteria which govern demands, which are valid or worthy not merely because they are wanted but because they are moral. These criteria, or evaluative principles, must always be preeminent to demand, for they are the distinguishing marks of a moral performance.

6. NORMATIVE POLITICAL THEORY

The description of a moral polity has been an exercise in normative inquiry, nothing more. A set of concepts "defining" morality has been used to describe a political society. If the account of morality is unacceptable, then so too will be the description of the moral polity, and in any case nothing exhaustive or definitive is claimed for this exercise. The lessons of the effort are more important than its success or failure. They are these: that normative inquiry is not paralyzed by the positivist thesis on values once the deficiencies of this thesis are revealed, and normative

---

[18]See, for example, David Easton, *A Systems Analysis of Political Life* (New York: John Wiley & Sons, Inc., 1965).

inquiry is as amenable to systematic or rigorous exploration as any of the empirical modes of political inquiry. It should be noticed that the practice in empirical science of defining two concepts, bringing them to bear on one another, and then naming the results, is no more or less than what we have done here in "fitting" the concept of morality to social arrangements.

This excursion into normative theory began with a discussion of neutrality in social inquiry. Very quickly it was demonstrated that claims for and against neutrality depend upon certain philosophical positions on language and the necessity of certain experiences. If we were to take a prospective look at normative political theory on the basis of where this discussion has led, the following possibilities occur. First, one can investigate claims, once commonly accepted in rationalist philosophy, that conditions can be identified which are necessary for certain kinds of experiences to occur, in the sense in which Kant asked this question of experience generally. In the context of normative political interests, the question is: What conditions are necessary for political or moral experience to occur, in the sense that if they are absent such experiences are impossible? This question can be posed either in the philosophy of language, or in phenomenology.[19] It is clear that if necessity can be demonstrated for experience, then the derivation of *ought* from *is* becomes more reasonable. Second, one can conceptualize evaluative systems and, like the exercise here, extend them to models of society. This reconstruction of normative systems is, in principle, a revival of the traditional concern in political theory for the ideal polity. It suggests that metatheoretical exercises, as in conceptualizing morality, can be effectively joined with substantive theoretical claims, as in describing the moral polity, a joining on normative terrain common in past theories of politics. Third, one can examine the feasibility of different social arrangements as means to the realization of specified moral goals, an examination that will encounter the incrementalist-holist dispute in policy implementation.

All three kinds of inquiry suggested above lead to many different kinds of theory, as certainly language philosophy and phenomenology can produce strikingly dissimilar results even with the same inquiry. But whatever the results, and however palatable the arguments in this book have been, it is undeniable that normative political theory is neither dead nor dying, but rather alive and rich with possibilities.

[19]See, for example, Noam Chomsky's revival of rationalist philosophy through a theory of language in *Cartesian Linguistics* (New York: Harper & Row, Publishers, 1966), and in the fuller statement of the theory, *Aspects of a Theory of Syntax* (Cambridge, Mass.: M.I.T. Press, 1965). See also Chomsky's *Language and Mind* (New York: Harcourt Brace Jovanovich, 1968). For an introduction to phenomenology in social analysis, the most readable presentation is Maurice Natason's *The Journeying Self* (Reading, Mass.: Addison-Wesley Publishing Co., Inc., 1970), plus Peter Winch's *The Idea of a Social Science*.

FOR FURTHER READING

Dahl, Robert, and Lindblom, Charles. *Politics, Economics, and Welfare.* New York: Harper & Row, Publishers, 1953.

Devlin, Patrick. *The Enforcement of Morals.* New York: Oxford University Press, 1970.

Hart, H. L. A. *Law, Liberty, and Morality.* New York: Random House, Inc., 1963.

Nagel, Ernest. "The Enforcement of Morals." *Humanist,* XXVIII (May-June 1968), 20–27.

Popper, Karl. *The Poverty of Historicism.* London: Routledge, Kegan, Paul, 1959.

————. *The Open Society and Its Enemies.* Vols. I & II. London: George Routledge & Sons, 1945.

Braybrooke, David, and Lindblom, Charles. *A Strategy of Decision.* New York: The Free Press, 1963.

Simon, Herbert. *Administrative Behavior.* New York: The Macmillan Company, 1959.

INDEX